Olivia Rodrigo

All American

The Illustrated Biography

EMILIE MURRAY

sona BOOKS

First published in the UK 2024 by Sona Books an imprint of Danann Media Publishing Ltd.

WARNING: For private domestic use only, any unauthorised Copying, hiring, lending or public performance of this book is illegal.

Prod Code: SON0558

Photography courtesy of

Getty images:

John Shearer/MTV VMAs 2021	Isaac Brekken	JMEnternational
Momodu Mansaray / Stringer	Jon Kopaloff	Noam Galai
Michael Tran	David Wolff-Patrick	Stephane Cardinale - Corbis
Frazer Harrison	Jim Dyson	Frazer Harrison / Staff
Jenny Anderson	Joseph Okpako	Gotham / Contributor
Kevin Winter	Ryan Kang	Rob Kim / Stringer
Kevin Mazur	Samir Hussein	
	Amy Sussman	

Alamy images:

Sipa US	Katrina Young	WENN Rights Ltd
ZUMA Press, Inc.	Barry King	Gerard Ferry
Associated Press	MediaPunch Inc	Richard Levine
Everett Collection Inc	UPI	

Other images Wiki Commons

Book layout & design by Audrey Alexander

All rights reserved. No Part of this title may be reproduced or transmitted in any material form (including photocopying or storing it in any medium by electronic means and whether or not transiently or incidentally to some other use of this publication) without the written permission of the copyright owner, except in accordance with the provisions of the Copyright, Designs and Patents Act 1988. Applications for the copyright owner's written permission should be addressed to the publisher.

This is an independent publication and it is unofficial and unauthorised and as such has no connection with the artist or artists featured, their management or any other organisation connected in any way whatsoever with the artist or artists featured in the book.

Made in EU.

ISBN: 978-1-915343-75-8

Contents

INTRODUCTION	09
THE EARLY YEARS...	12
THE DISNEY YEARS...	18
AND SO IT BEGINS...	26
DRIVERS LICENSE	32
SOUR: THE ALBUM	40
SOUR TOUR	58
LIFE AFTER SOUR	70
GUTS: THE ALBUM	86
GUTS SPILLED	104
GUTS TOUR	114
STYLE ICON	134
OUTRO	140

Olivia Rodrigo performing at her sold-out *GUTS* World Tour, 2024

Introduction

Olivia Rodrigo burst onto the global music scene with the kind of impact that often seems reserved for overnight sensations. With the release of her debut single "drivers license" in January 2021, she quickly became a household name, dominating charts and streaming platforms, and capturing the hearts of millions with her deeply personal and evocative lyrics. However, beneath this meteoric rise lies a story of relentless dedication and passion, through a decade-long journey that began far from the bright lights of stardom.

Long before Olivia's voice echoed through the speakers of fans worldwide, she was a young girl with a dream, penning her first songs in the quiet sanctuary of her bedroom. These early compositions, crafted away from the public eye, were the foundation upon which she built her burgeoning career.

Born on February 20, 2003, in Murrieta, California, Olivia's love for music was evident from a very young age. By the time she was five, she was already participating in singing and acting classes, clearly bitten by the showbiz bug.

Olivia's big break came when she landed two roles on Disney Channel, giving her a platform to showcase not only her talents as a young actress, but also as a performer. Her gift for songwriting was evident from the get-go, and her star power even more so, and Olivia quickly caught the attention of record producers. All the songs she wrote in her room for all those years, as a hobby, were now inching her closer to her lifelong dream.

In January 2021, the release of her debut single "drivers license" marked a watershed moment in her career. While the COVID-19 pandemic was still spreading across the globe, Olivia Rodrigo was becoming the most famous teenager in the entertainment industry. Her debut single, quickly went viral, shattering streaming records and earning critical acclaim. She swiftly continued her momentum when she released her debut album SOUR in May 2021, cementing her status as a pop powerhouse. Olivia's music often delves into themes of heartbreak, identity, and growing up, striking a chord with listeners of all ages, demonstrating her remarkable ability to translate personal experiences into universal anthems. Tracks like "good 4 u" and "deja vu" highlighted her versatility, blending different genres from pop-punk to indie rock, all while maintaining a sound that was distinctly her own.

Olivia Rodrigo's story is a testament to the power of persistence and the importance of nurturing one's passions. It is a reminder that true success is often built on a foundation of quiet, unseen effort.

This book will explore the life, career, and impact of Olivia Rodrigo, delving into the stories behind her music, her rise to fame, and the ways in which she continues to influence and inspire.

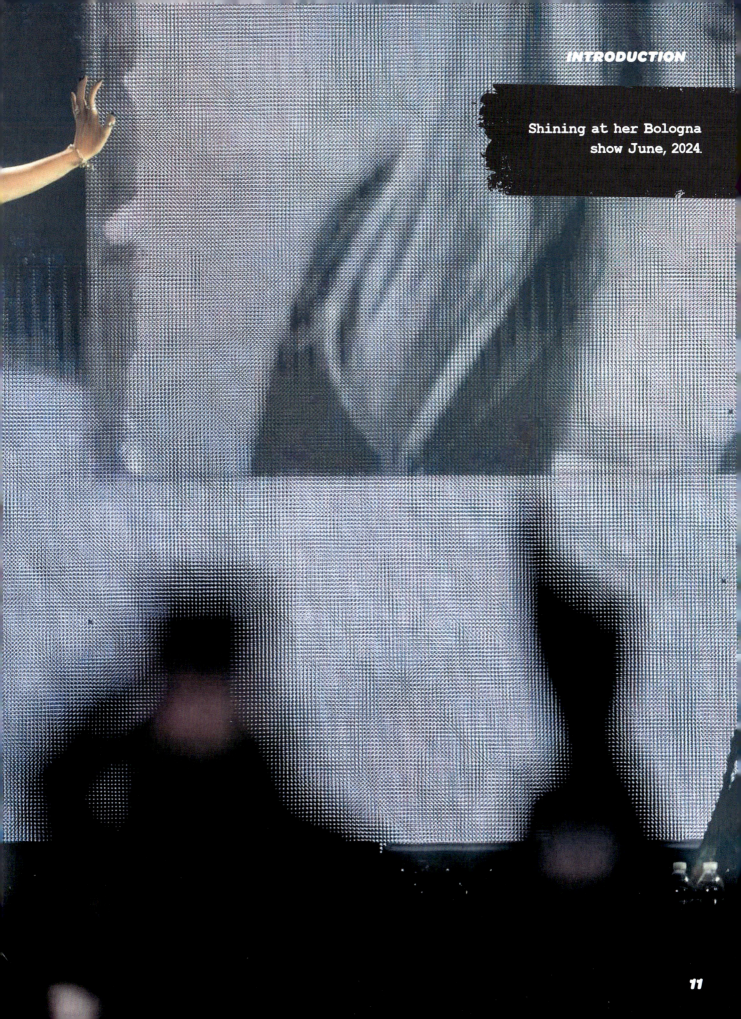

INTRODUCTION

Shining at her Bologna show June, 2024.

The Early Years...

Olivia Isabel Rodrigo was born on the 20th of February 2003, in Murrieta, California, to Jennifer, a schoolteacher, and Chris, a family therapist. As an only child, she grew up in the neighbouring town Temecula, "the suburbs of all suburbs," as she once described it.

It didn't take long for Olivia's parents to recognise that their only daughter was a superstar in the making. Before she could even string sentences together, the future pop princess was already composing songs – even if they were about her pet snake, Stripes. She has subsequently mentioned in interviews that she first got the snake when she was just three years old and even brought him to her preschool for show and tell. She says that people are usually afraid when they hear she has a snake, but her schoolmates were fans. They let Stripes slither through their hands and talked about him a lot afterward. Olivia jokes that she became the coolest kid in school that day, and everyone remembered her because of her special pet snake.

At the age of five, Olivia's parents signed her up for singing lessons with Jennifer Dustman, who would begin to enrol the kindergartener into local singing competitions. Under the advisement of Dustman, Olivia's parents quickly signed her up for acting lessons as well. Olivia also picked up piano lessons at the age of nine. Although she was seemingly set up to become a rising star, Olivia had other aspirations. Her first career dream was to become an Olympic gymnast, which she has later admitted wouldn't have been the right fit. "I was terrible at it – terrible" she said of her first dream.

Despite not wanting to be a songwriter right away, the origins for it have always been there... ever since she was a little girl Olivia was in love with music. At home, Olivia would sing all the time, belting out choruses from her parents' favourite bands - "Seven Nation Army" by The White Stripes and "Bathwater" by No Doubt. The Disney Channel star also mentioned that her first gigs were to see the punk band Weezer, The Cure and The Smashing Pumpkins. Although there's no doubt she was influenced by her parents' taste in music, there were three female singer-songwriters that inspired her the most: Taylor Swift, Lorde, and Alanis Morissette.

THE EARLY YEARS

Attending P.S. ARTS Presents Express Yourself, 2015

Olivia Rodrigo ALL AMERICAN

Influences

Alanis Morissette

ALANIS MORISETTE

Alanis Morissette (born June 1, 1974, Ottawa, Ontario, Canada) is a Canadian musician known for her confessional lyrics and a layered rock-influenced sound. Her 1995 album Jagged Little Pill established her as one of alternative rock's foremost female vocalists of the 1990s. During an artist-on-artist interview with Rolling Stone, Olivia told Alanis Morissette just how much her music awakened her songwriting side. "I remember having my mind blown when I was 13. I was in the car with my parents listening to *Jagged Little Pill*. I remember hearing 'Perfect,' and I was like, 'Oh, my God.' I told my music teacher a couple days after: 'You can write songs like that?' I just looked at music and songwriting in a completely different way."s

The pair have maintained a close friendship since they first met at the Rolling Stone interview in October 2021, with Olivia even honouring Alanis at the Canadian Songwriters Hall of Fame a year later. In her speech, Olivia detailed the influence Alanis had on her craft, saying "My life was completely changed. Alanis' songwriting was unlike anything I'd ever heard before and I haven't heard anything quite like it since. And that voice – fierce and tender and sometimes funny and playful. I became hooked for life."

She continued: "Alanis captured the anger, the grief and the love of the human experience better than anyone. Her songs unite people and empower people and help them heal. Alanis, you're a trailblazer and you've inspired an entire generation of uncompromising, radically honest songwriting".

Not only did Rodrigo befriend one of her musical inspirations, she would also have the chance to share the stage with Alanis and perform a rendition of her iconic song "You Oughta Know" on the SOUR tour.

THE EARLY YEARS

Taylor Swift

On Valentine's Day Sunday 2021, Olivia Rodrigo co-hosted Apple Music 1's The Travis Mills Show and revealed just how much she adores Taylor Swift.

"I would just love to just be in a studio with Taylor," she told the host. "I don't even have to write with her. I just want to watch how she does it because I just think she's such a genius." And when Mills, mentioned a possible collaboration with the "Cruel Summer" singer Rodrigo said, "That's the dream, she's totally my biggest idol and biggest songwriting inspiration". In another interview, Olivia recalled how long she has been a Swifty saying, "I've looked up to Taylor since I was five years old. Obviously, I think Taylor's the best songwriter of all time," "I think her writing every single one of her songs was a big inspiration for me. I take songwriting the most seriously out of any career that I have. It's just so important to me. And I think that's sort of the same with her. I'm like, the biggest fangirl."

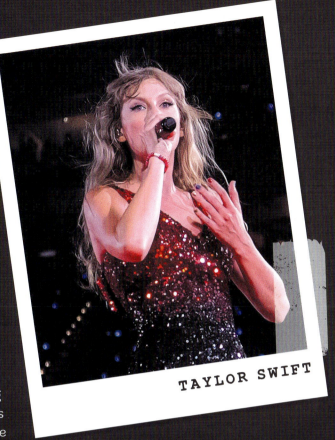
TAYLOR SWIFT

Taylor has also shown her support for the budding young artist and even sent Olivia a handwritten letter congratulating her on her newfound success.

"I don't want to divulge too much because it's really sweet and personal, but she talks a lot about how, I think, you make your own luck in the world," Rodrigo told Billboard. "And when you do kind things to others, good things come your way."

Lorde

Lorde's impact on Olivia extends far beyond just lyrics and production. "I just like Lorde in general I guess," Olivia previously told MTV. "I remember going to her Melodrama Tour a couple of years ago with my friends. And like, walking out of the Staples Center and being so moved. I just remember that being such an experience. And being like, 'Woah. That's how art changes you.' I felt like a changed person. I wanna make art like that. I wanna make art like Lorde."

Olivia Rodrigo ALL AMERICAN

LORDE

In a 2024 roundtable interview with The Hollywood Reporter featuring several of the year's prominent songwriters, Olivia revealed how the "trajectory" of her life was changed upon hearing Lorde's 2013 hit, "Royals."

"I remember getting my first phone at probably, like, 12 or 13, and the first thing I did was download Lorde, *'Pure Heroin'*, I love that record so much," continued Rodrigo. "I remember listening to it as I first started writing songs and just being blown away by her lyrics that are just about, you know, being a teenager, living in the suburbs."

At the time, the New Zealand native was only 16 when she released her debut album *Pure Heroine* in 2013. "She made being young and doing these seemingly unimportant things feel so sacred and beautiful" confessed Olivia.

Despite her natural talent for music, and the strong female singers she had to look up to, Olivia always felt that she didn't look like any of her idols.

Olivia is Filipino-American through her father's side of the family. She has frequently spoken admiringly about her great-grandfather's immigration to the United States and continues to celebrate her heritage in her own life.

"My dad grew up in a house where they were always making Filipino food, his grandpa always spoke Tagalog. All of those traditions have trickled down to our generation. Every Thanksgiving, we have lumpia, and things like that," Olivia told The Center for Asian American Media (CAAM) back in 2018.

Even though she loves her roots, she also acknowledged that growing up without many mixed-race role models took a toll on her confidence.

"It's hard for anyone to grow up in this media where it feels like if you don't have European features and blonde hair and blue eyes, you're not traditionally pretty," said Olivia. "I felt that a lot – since I don't look exactly like the girl next door, I'm not attractive. That actually took me a while to shake off. It's something I'm still shaking of now."

To deal with the lack of Filipino representation, Olivia did what she did best and started writing songs.

THE EARLY YEARS

Naive Girl

"I think the first proper song I ever wrote – the first one I finessed and that was a complete song – I was probably about 12 or 13. It was called 'Naive Girl' and I put it on my Instagram. It's probably still out there somewhere, in the depths of the internet." Some of the lyrics of the song include "My education is built upon some 20th century daydream, I'm beginning to learn, despite the façade, that people are not always as pretty as they seem," followed by the chorus of "Little naive girl isn't so naive anymore."

Pretty impressive for a 12-year-old!

It was also around this time that Olivia got her first big break and made her acting debut portraying the lead role of Grace Thomas in the direct-to-video film *An American Girl: Grace Stirs Up Success*. A year later, the 12-year-old landed the role in Disney Channel's Bizaardvark in 2016, playing a vlogger for which she learned to play the guitar and relocated her family to Los Angeles.

The Disney Years...

Bizaardvark is an American comedy television series created by Kyle Stegina and Josh Lehrman that premiered on Disney Channel on June 24, 2016. The show ran for three seasons, totalling 63 episodes, with its final episode airing on April 13, 2019. The series stars Madison Hu, Olivia Rodrigo, Jake Paul, DeVore Ledridge, Ethan Wacker, Maxwell Simkins, and Elie Samouhi. In addition to the regular episodes, the series also featured shorts titled Bizaardvark Shorts.

Bizaardvark!!!

The series revolves around two 12-year-old best friends, Frankie Wong (played by Madison Hu) and Paige Olvera (played by Olivia Rodrigo), who write funny songs and create music videos for their online channel, titled Bizaardvark, a portmanteau of the words "bizarre" and "aardvark". When they hit 10,000 subscribers, they are accepted into the Vuuugle studios, where the amateur musicians get to work from a creative studio space that they hope will take their videos to the next level. In their cool new environment, and with the help of family and friends, the girls will embark on a series of comedic adventures in their quest to become online stars.

THE DISNEY YEARS

Real life Besties

Olivia Rodrigo and Madison Hu took their on-screen friendship off screen during their time on the Disney Channel series Bizaardvark. Spending three seasons together, they formed a deep bond through countless hours of rehearsing lines, filming scenes, and navigating the complexities of being young actresses in the spotlight. Their camaraderie was particularly evident in a "Best Friend Tag" video for Disney Channel. Olivia and Madison's friendship extended well beyond their Disney Channel years, evolving from co-stars to lifelong pals. After "Bizaardvark," they continued to support each other's careers and personal growth, frequently seen celebrating milestones and attending events together. Their bond remained strong through various life changes, with both friends often mentioning each other in interviews and on social media.

Olivia Rodrigo ALL AMERICAN

Olivia was cast in Bizaardvark at the young age of 12, and often reflects upon her experience in interviews. She refers to her co-star Madison Hu, who plays Frankie, as her "soulmate." Despite this close bond, she described life as a Disney star, especially at such a young age, as potentially isolating. "It's a multicamera sitcom, so literally every set is within a yard of each other," she told the magazine. "You just walk to the different sets."

When she was 14, Rodrigo experienced "an identity crisis on steroids," leading her to ask herself some profound questions: "Who the fuck am I? Who cares about me? How do I treat people?" Due to her career, she often found herself in unusual situations, ones that most people her age don't typically face: "Most 14-year-olds aren't in a room with adults being like, 'So, what's your brand?'"

Although filming Bizaardvark was a lonely time for her, Olivia had already started to discover her passion, songwriting, a skill that would certainly help her get her next acting gig.

High School Musical: The Musical: The Series

"High School Musical: The Musical: The Series" (HSMTMTS) premiered on Disney+ in November 2019, offering a fresh, meta take on the beloved "High School Musical" franchise. Created by Tim Federle, this mockumentary-style series introduces a new generation of high school students navigating the complexities of teenage life while paying homage to the original films that captured the hearts of millions.

The series stars Olivia Rodrigo, Joshua Bassett, Matt Cornett, Sofia Wylie, Larry Saperstein, Julia Lester, Dara Reneé, Frankie Rodriguez, Mark St. Cyr, Kate Reinders, Joe Serafini, Saylor Bell Curda, Adrian Lyles, and Liamani Segura. Olivia was cast in the lead role of Nini Salazar-Roberts, a talented and ambitious high school student navigating her way through personal and artistic growth.

The show has been praised for its inclusive and diverse cast, authentic portrayal of teenage issues, and its ability to balance nostalgia with modern storytelling. The chemistry among the

THE DISNEY YEARS

cast members, particularly between Rodrigo and Bassett, has been a highlight, driving much of the series' emotional and dramatic arcs.

Olivia Rodrigo's portrayal of Nini Salazar-Roberts in HSMTMTS cemented her as one of the most talented and promising young performers of her generation. Her portrayal of Nini resonated with audiences and critics alike, showcasing Rodrigo's multifaceted talents in acting, singing, and songwriting.

HSMTMTS

Set at a fictionalized version of East High School, where the original "High School Musical" movies were filmed, the first season follows a group of teenage theatre enthusiasts participating in a staging of "High School Musical: The Musical" as their school production. Each subsequent season features a different musical and delves into the lives of the characters as they navigate friendships, love, personal interests, identity, and family relationships. In the second season, the theatre students take on a production of "Beauty and the Beast" for their spring musical. Under the guidance of their passionate drama teacher, Miss Jenn, played by Kate Reinders, they aim to win a prestigious local student theatre competition. The season introduces new challenges as they compete against their rival school, North High, adding a layer of tension and excitement. Departing from the usual school setting, the third season is set at Camp Shallow Lake, a summer theatre camp in California. The students prepare a stage production of "Frozen" while a documentary series captures their rehearsal process over the summer.

Olivia Rodrigo ALL AMERICAN

Olivia Rodrigo and the cast of 'High School Musical: The Musical: The Series' at the Disney+ premiere, Burbank, California 2019

THE DISNEY YEARS

All I Want

"All I Want" was written by Olivia for her character, Nini, in the fourth episode of HSMTMTS. In the context of the show, Nini writes and performs the song as she grapples with her feelings about her ex-boyfriend Ricky Bowen, played by Joshua Bassett, and her new romantic interest, E.J. Caswell, played by Matt Cornett. The song captures Nini's emotional turmoil and desire for a genuine, uncomplicated love, reflecting the universal teenage experience of navigating complex relationships.

The music video for "All I Want" features Rodrigo performing the song in various locations around East High, interspersed with scenes from the series that highlight Nini's emotional journey. The video complements the song's themes and has garnered millions of views on YouTube.

Upon its release, "All I Want" quickly gained traction on streaming platforms, amassing millions of streams and earning a spot on the Billboard Hot 100 chart. The song's popularity extended beyond the show's fanbase, appealing to a wider audience and showcasing Olivia's broad appeal.

The song quickly gained traction, going viral on TikTok and capturing the hearts of viewers worldwide. This success played a pivotal role in Rodrigo's career trajectory.

Joshua Bassett and Olivia Rodrigo perform at the 5th Annual Elsie Fest: Broadway's Outdoor Music Festival, New York City, 2019

Olivia Rodrigo live at The Theatre at Ace Hotel, Los Angeles, 2023

And so it begins...

Olivia Rodrigo initially gained prominence as an actress, notably starring in the Disney Channel series "Bizaardvark."

However, it was her role as Nini Salazar-Roberts in the immensely popular Disney+ show "High School Musical: The Musical: The Series" that catapulted her to household name status in 2019. It was during this time that Rodrigo first showcased her song writing abilities when she penned the original song "All I Want", which her character performed in the show's first season, leading to a record deal and marking her official transition into the music industry.

Who is Dan Nigro?

Before teaming up with one of the world's biggest pop stars, Nigro kickstarted his music career as the lead singer and guitarist for indie rock band, As Tall As Lions. They released three albums and three Eps together from 2002 to 2009, before disbanding in 2010. Prior to working with Rodrigo, the New York native made his first major break as a songwriter by co-writing several tracks on Sky Ferreira's critically acclaimed debut album, "Night Time, My Time". This success led him to collaborate with artists such as Kylie Minogue, Billy Idol, Carly Rae Jepsen, Lewis Capaldi, and more.

Olivia Rodrigo ALL AMERICAN

The pair met after Nigro saw a video of Olivia singing her song "Happier" on Instagram, where he was instantly blown away by her talent and sent her a DM. Their official introduction occurred later on, when members of Olivia's team at Interscope Records arranged a meeting in March 2020, a week before the world came to a standstill. The COVID-19 pandemic halted their plans but a couple of months later, as lockdown restrictions softened, the duo were finally able to hunker down in Nigro's home studio and start working on new material.

Dan and Olivia share the same mindset of bringing in an idea and working together to make it better. In an interview with Variety, the pair talked about their writing process, with Olivia offering raw talent to the table and Dan matching it with a "keen ear for clean and creative production". "I think the balance lies in the fact that Olivia is so lyric-focused, while I'm more melody and texture-focused," Nigro said of their collaboration process. "Her main objective while we're working on each song is making sure that every word hits exactly how it needs to, while I obsess over each chord and which inversion of it to play, or how much low-end to introduce when a chorus hits to make sure the impact is right without taking away from the vocal performance".

Olivia also commented on her co-writer, saying "He just kind of takes my songs and elevates them and polishes them up and makes them better".

One of the "half baked" song ideas Olivia brought to Dan at the beginning of their relationship was "drivers license", a song that would later change both their lives forever. And thus, their sonic partnership was born.

Dan Nigro and Olivia Rodrigo celebrating Grammy wins at the 64th Annual Awards, Las Vegas, 2022

AND SO IT BEGINS...

AND SO IT BEGINS...

Fans at the 2021 iHeartRadio Music Festival, Las Vegas, 2018

"drivers license"

The inspiration behind Olivia's debut hit single came from a true story in which she drove around her suburban town, listening to sad music and crying over a recent breakup.

When she got home, she decided to write about her experience while, as she has self-professed, literally crying on her living room floor. During her song writing process, Olivia came across a diary entry dated July 13, 2020, with the first line reading "I got my drivers license today, a very highly anticipated achievement", a sentence that would later inspire the opening lyrics to "drivers license". She subsequently revealed in her documentary "Driving Home 2 U", released in 2022, that the entry continued with "all my relatives called to congratulate me. I realized part of the reason I wanted to get my license so bad was because of... this boy", purposely omitting the name of the boy in question. Though never confirmed, there was a lot of speculation that the boy she mentioned was none other than Joshua Bassett.

"DRIVERS LICENSE"

Joshua Bassett (2019- 2020)

Olivia Rodrigo and Joshua Bassett at the after party for Disney+'s 'High School Musical: The Musical: The Series' premiere, Burbank, California 2019

Joshua Bassett is an American singer/ songwriter and actor. The pair met back in 2019 when they both starred alongside each other on the set of High School Musical: The Musical: The Series. Rodrigo, then 16, and Bassett, then 18, played love interests on the show, and rumours quickly began to swirl that the two young actors had taken their on-screen romance, off-screen. Their relationship was short lived though, only lasting several months, as the couple eventually called it quits in the summer of 2020. Their dalliance undoubtedly left a mark on Olivia, as her experience with Joshua became the catalyst for "drivers license" and many other songs off her soon to be released album, SOUR. But drama was right around the corner, as Joshua was spotted with fellow singer/ songwriter Sabrina Carpenter just days after his split from Olivia.

Olivia Rodrigo ALL AMERICAN

Disney Love Triangle

"drivers license" was released as Olivia Rodrigo's lead single off her debut album *SOUR*, on January 8th, 2021. The song was an instant hit, quickly topping the charts and breaking records, but it also served as an impetus for a series of love triangle rumours between herself, Joshua Bassett and Disney Channel alumnus, Sabrina Carpenter.

Olivia's lyric in 'drivers license', where she mentions a "blonde girl", had fans speculating about its inspiration, particularly after the demo version of the song surfaced in which the original lyric was 'brunette girl'. So, what inspired the change?

Sabrina Carpenter

Sabrina Carpenter is an American singer/ songwriter, best known for her role as Maya Hart in Disney Channel's spinoff series 'Girl Meets World' as well as for her music career. She first got embroiled in "drivers license" drama when she was seen with Joshua at a Black Lives Matter protest, confirming the split rumours between him and Olivia.

SABRINA CARPENTER

"DRIVERS LICENSE"

Sabrina then appeared in Joshua's music video for his song "Anyone Else", released in July of 2020, where the pair were filmed holding hands at the back of a car. A couple of weeks later, they were pictured having lunch together in Studio City, California. It wasn't until October 2020, when Sabrina posted a video of Joshua and herself both dressed up for Halloween as Shark Boy and Lava Girl, that fans began to suspect a romance between the two artists.

Soon after the release of "drivers license," Joshua Bassett came out with his own single titled "Lie Lie Lie" on January 14th 2020, fuelling more and more rumours of a love triangle.

Joshua used the single to call out a person who was "acting all so innocent" as they spoke poorly of him. In the music video, Bassett is seen driving alone in a car, a possible nod to Olivia's clip for "drivers license".

Although many people believed that "Lie Lie Lie" was a direct response to Olivia Rodrigo's explosive track, Joshua has since come out and set the record straight, writing "I wrote 'Lie, Lie, Lie' after I found out a friend had been lying about me behind my back for a long time," on his Instagram story.

The drama further escalated when Sabrina Carpenter released her song "Skin" at the end of January, the same month as "drivers license" and "Lie Lie Lie" came out. In "Skin," Sabrina seemed to be addressing the rumours surrounding her involvement in the situation, asserting her own perspective.

The first verse of the song mentions that maybe the two girls could've been friends in another life and even goes on to mention that maybe "blonde" was only a rhyme, referring of course to "blonde girl" from Olivia's song. The song definitely seems to be a response to Olivia's "drivers license", or at least that's what fans have taken it as.

All three artists had their music dissected and personal lives scrutinised for all to see. Fans even picked sides, defending their favourite artist at the expense of the others.

Though the love triangle fiasco proved to be quite messy, Olivia and Joshua have managed to remain amicable, and were even seen posing and laughing together on the red carpet for the premiere of High School Musical: The Musical: The Series season three in 2022.

Olivia Rodrigo ALL AMERICAN

But beyond the gossip, "drivers license" hit the jackpot when it found itself the centre of a viral TikTok trend. Started by TikTok user Mel Sommers, she re-created a scene from Rodrigo's music video in which she falls back away from the camera during a dramatic shift between the verse and chorus. The trend quickly gained momentum, with countless users participating and sharing their own interpretations of the scene. Many of these TikTok videos garnered millions of views and likes, breathing new life into the song's streaming numbers, significantly boosting its popularity, and contributing to its success on the music charts.

"DRIVERS LICENSE"

Breaking Records

"drivers license" debuted at the top of the Billboard Hot 100, giving Rodrigo her first number-one single in the United States. It also marked her second entry on the chart, after 'All I Want'.

Billboard reported that, in its first three days in the US, the song sold over 16,000 digital downloads and received more than 21 million streams. Compared to its release day, the song's total streams increased by 122% on its second day, and rose another 32% in its third day.

The song reached number one on international Spotify, Apple Music and Amazon Music songs charts. The song broke the Spotify record for most one-day streams for a non-holiday song, with over 15 million global streams on its fourth day (January 11, 2021).

"drivers license" then went on to break the Spotify record for most streams of a song in a single week, with over 65 million streams in the week ending January 14, 2021. And to top it all off, it also broke the record for fastest song to reach 100 million streams on Spotify.

Olivia won a slew of awards including one Grammy and two MTV awards.

64th Annual GRAMMY Awards, Las Vegas, 2022

Olivia Rodrigo ALL AMERICAN

"drivers license" masterfully captures the whirlwind emotions of young love and the pain of seeing an ex move on with someone new. From the opening sound of keys in a car ignition, to the emotional belts of the chorus, "drivers license" articulates the bittersweetness of growing up. Olivia Rodrigo delicately balances the exhilaration of newfound freedom, in this case obtaining her driver's license, and the lingering ache of a broken heart. In her documentary "driving home 2 u", Olivia talked about how excited she was at the prospect of getting her license as it was going to make her feel less like a kid next to her older boyfriend. "drivers license" transcends its status as a mere pop song, serving as a poignant reflection on the complexities of love, loss, and the journey towards self-discovery. It resonates deeply with listeners of all ages, capturing the universal experience of navigating the messy business of the affairs of the heart.

But "drivers license" was only the beginning, Olivia Rodrigo was on track to becoming one of the biggest pop stars in the world with the release of her upcoming debut album *SOUR*.

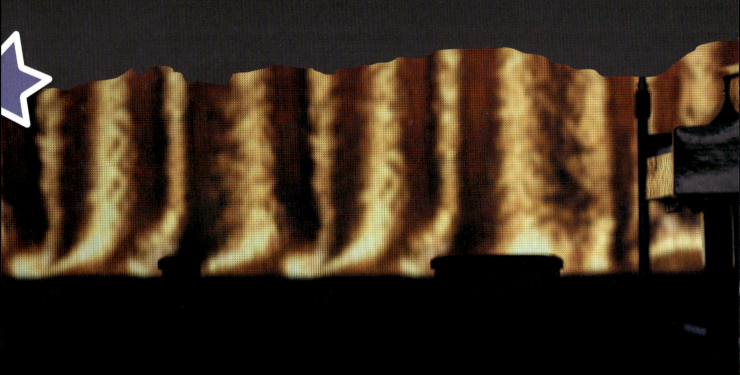

Olivia on the Daytime Stage at the 2021 iHeartRadio Music Festival, Las Vegas

"DRIVERS LICENSE"

SOUR: the album

Tracklist

brutal

traitor

drivers license

1 step forward, 3 steps back

deja vu

good 4 u

enough for you

happier

jealousy, jealousy

favorite crime

hope ur ok

SOUR: THE ALBUM

At only 18 years old, Olivia shattered records and defied expectations in the music industry.

Even in a world where streaming's rise means chart records are broken all the time, the debut single by the Disney star was an anomaly – and her debut album *SOUR* wasn't any different. *SOUR*, written entirely by Rodrigo and producer Daniel Nigro, deals with all the emotions that comes with being a teenage girl with none of the meaningless word salad that popstars often hide behind. Olivia fearlessly wears her heart on her sleeve, unafraid to tell her truth or even be a tad bit vexing. The young singer has expressed pride in the album's focus on emotions that are often deemed socially unacceptable for girls, such as anger, jealousy, spite, and sadness. The title itself reclaims the word 'sour,' which typically carries connotations of bitterness and undesirability, often used to criticize women. In a world where girls are often taught to avoid scaring men with their big emotions, writing an entire album about the fury and heartache of being forgotten by an ex might seem ill-advised. Yet, it's precisely these shades of vulnerability that make *SOUR* so cathartic and charming.

Despite the album being decidedly teenage, Olivia's ability to turn very specific feelings into a simple song makes her a universally appreciated pop star.

Breaking Records

Olivia made history as the first ever new artist to have her first three singles debut in the top 10 back to back on the Billboard charts.

Her debut album, *SOUR*, opened at No. 1 on the Billboard 200 chart with 8 of the top 10 songs on the Streaming Songs chart, breaking a record held by Taylor Swift since August of 2020.

Performing at the 2021 MTV Video Music Awards, New York City

SOUR: THE ALBUM

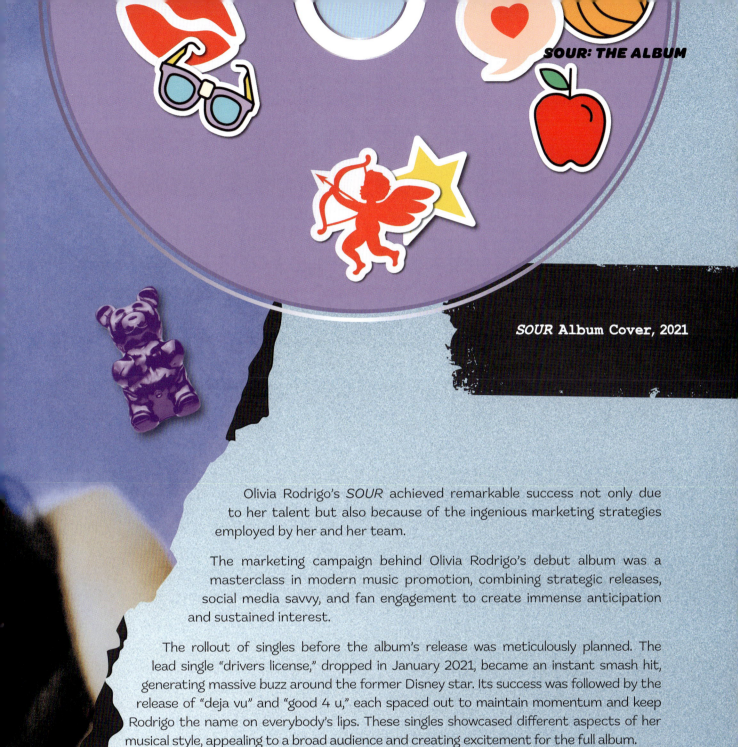

SOUR: THE ALBUM

SOUR Album Cover, 2021

Olivia Rodrigo's *SOUR* achieved remarkable success not only due to her talent but also because of the ingenious marketing strategies employed by her and her team.

The marketing campaign behind Olivia Rodrigo's debut album was a masterclass in modern music promotion, combining strategic releases, social media savvy, and fan engagement to create immense anticipation and sustained interest.

The rollout of singles before the album's release was meticulously planned. The lead single "drivers license," dropped in January 2021, became an instant smash hit, generating massive buzz around the former Disney star. Its success was followed by the release of "deja vu" and "good 4 u," each spaced out to maintain momentum and keep Rodrigo the name on everybody's lips. These singles showcased different aspects of her musical style, appealing to a broad audience and creating excitement for the full album.

But probably the most impactful marketing strategy employed by Olivia and her team is in the art direction of the album. *SOUR*'s distinctive aesthetic, which is very reminiscent of the late 90's and early 00's era, made her brand very recognisable. From the iconic use of the colour purple to the stickers plastered on her face and the grungy Y2K outfits, there really seems to be no aspect of the *SOUR* universe not touched by Olivia's personal tastes. Rodrigo's heavy involvement in the promotion of her album made the campaign incredibly genuine and relatable to her fans, resulting in a high level of fan engagement.

In addition, the distinctive brand of *SOUR* also allowed for some very innovative partnerships.

Olivia Rodrigo **ALL AMERICAN**

Olivia Rodrigo X Sour Patch Kids

"First they're sour, then they're sweet"

Olivia Rodrigo's collaboration with Sour Patch Kids is a standout example of how strategic brand partnerships can enhance an album release. On May 21st 2021, Olivia brought out her own customised, limited edition Sour Patch Kids, in her iconic shade of purple. This partnership was particularly fitting, given the album's themes of youthful angst and heartbreak, which resonated well with the playful yet slightly mischievous brand identity of Sour Patch Kids - and her album is called Sour after all. They celebrated the launch by putting together pop-up stores up and down America, where fans could go and buy Sour sweets along with exclusive *SOUR* merchandise.

By creating special edition products, immersive experiences, and engaging social media content, the campaign effectively promoted *SOUR* while providing added value to fans. This partnership not only boosted Rodrigo's album visibility but also reinforced her connection with her audience in a fun and innovative way.

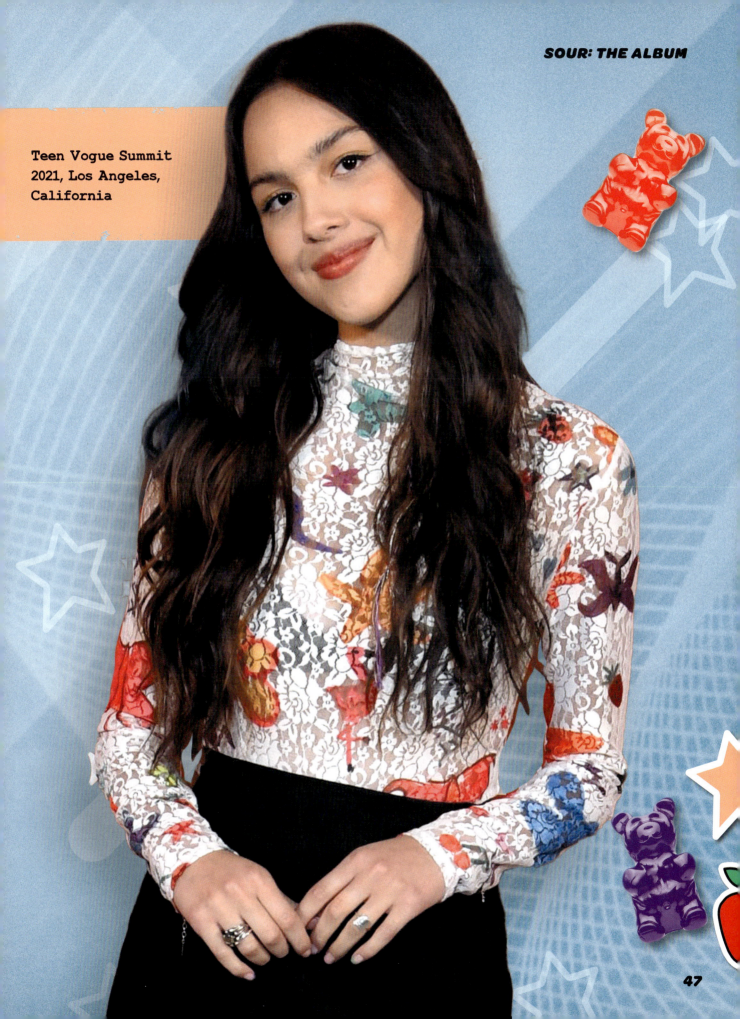

Teen Vogue Summit 2021, Los Angeles, California

SOUR: THE ALBUM

SOUR Prom

Another creative expansion of the *SOUR* universe was the release of Olivia Rodrigo's concert film *SOUR Prom*, on the 29th of June 2021. Rodrigo had just graduated from high school two weeks before the film's premiere, mentioning in interviews that her rise as one of pop's biggest stars often coincided with completing her statistics homework.

Due to work obligations surrounding her album release, the young singer had to sit out her real prom. Determined to not let it get her down, Olivia decided to throw a prom themed album release party and share the experience with her fans. She invited a group of them to a premiere event, even personally delivering invitations to some.

On the day of the premiere, Rodrigo and her guests gathered on a rooftop adorned with prom decorations, a drive-through photo booth, and a stage where she performed "traitor" and "good 4 u" live. Fans were able to take photos with Olivia and were treated to a bag of gifts to take home, and of course, got to view *SOUR Prom* on release.

The 27-minute cinematic piece features live performances of tracks from the *SOUR* album, set against various prom-themed backdrops with limousines, punch bowls, and slow dancing all making an appearance. Unlike traditional concert films, *SOUR Prom* was filmed without a live audience, resembling an extended music video spanning multiple tracks.

This creative choice offered a unique experience for fans worldwide, compensating for the lack of live concerts during covid times, and cementing Olivia Rodrigo as a pop superstar.

SOUR: THE ALBUM

Prom Queen Drama

The controversy between Olivia Rodrigo and Courtney Love emerged in June 2021 when Love accused Rodrigo of copying the cover art from her band, Hole's, 1994 album *Live Through This*, for the *SOUR Prom* promotional materials. Both images depict a prom queen with smeared makeup holding a bouquet of flowers. Love took to social media to express her discontent, suggesting that Olivia had used the concept without proper credit or acknowledgment.

Love initially posted the Sour Prom image on Instagram with the caption, "Spot the difference! #twinning", tagging Olivia Rodrigo. She then followed up with some additional, more direct comments on her Facebook saying, "it was rude of her, and geffen not to ask myself or Ellen von unwerth. It's happened my whole career so I d c. But manners is manners!". Geffen Records is Rodrigo's current record label, and Unwerth was the photographer behind the cover of *Live Through This*.

Olivia Rodrigo responded to Love's post by commenting, "love u and live through this sooooo much," acknowledging her admiration for Love and Hole's work. However, she did not explicitly address the issue of alleged plagiarism or copying. Instead, she posted a series of inspiration photos on her Instagram story, including stills from the film *Carrie*, which famously portrays an iconic prom queen.

Track by Track Analysis

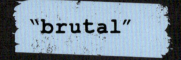
"brutal"

The opening track of the album immediately lets listeners know that there is no putting Olivia Rodrigo in a box. "brutal" is a rebellious pop punk anthem that sounds like a lovechild between Alanis Morissette's "You Oughta Know" and Elvis Costello's "Pump It Up". This song is decidedly teenage, in the best possible way, as the lyrics read like a stream of consciousness of all of Olivia's grievances. It's a blistering critique of every adolescent cliché, scrutinized and reshaped to reflect the chaotic contradictions of growing up in the social conditions that define Gen Z. Olivia evokes how pop culture tends to romanticise youth and how the teenage experience isn't always as glamourous as it may seem. The media frequently sells an idealized version of adolescence, particularly when depicting the lives of teenage girls. She even mentions how she can't even parallel park, a very universal sentiment indeed. She also references her insecurity, the public love triangle she was thrust into, and struggles with her ever-growing spotlight.

"brutal" was one of five music videos from her album *SOUR*, and one of four collaborations with director Petra Collins. The music video is just as angsty as the song, with Olivia Rodrigo decked out in fishnet tights, black combat boots and an Avril Lavigne-esque plaid two-piece set.

"traitor"

The second song on the album is a complete one-eighty from her previous track "brutal", as Olivia trades in her studs and chains for a slower tempo, melancholic ballad. This contrast on paper might seem like it would make for an inconsistent album, but it does quite the opposite. "traitor", for one, highlights her versatility as a songwriter and vocalist, while continuing to highlight the rollercoaster of emotions that comes with being a teen. One minute you're full of rage-fuelled angst, and the next you're crying on the bedroom floor over a breakup. "traitor" is for the latter times, which makes sense because according to Olivia Rodrigo, she wrote "traitor" in her bedroom after a breakup. She said, "I was really obsessed with this idea that somebody could be so close to you and then just turn around and be with somebody else so quickly. And I think that's such a universal thing that people go through".

SOUR: THE ALBUM

"traitor" is a deeply personal song and almost feels like reading a page from her diary, which is very reminiscent of Taylor Swift's confessional style of songwriting. Coupled with vocals that perfectly showcase her raw emotion, "traitor" is sure to be a breakup song classic.

"traitor" also got the music video treatment, this time directed by Olivia Bee. Rodrigo is filmed with friends at the back of a pick-up truck, playing in an arcade and swimming in a pool. During these typically fun activities, the viewer can see that the young singer is detached from the fun her friends are having. She is caught up in her own feelings of heartbreak that she passionately illustrates within the song.

"drivers license"

Very few songs over the last few years have had as much cultural significance as "drivers license" had in 2021. Apart from breaking a load of records and winning a good smattering of awards, "drivers license" truly solidified Olivia Rodrigo as a superstar in the making. In her debut single, Olivia masterfully captures the bittersweet journey of growing up, navigating love, and dealing with loss.

The track begins with a simple piano accompaniment, which gradually builds with subtle synths and a steady drumbeat until it all crescendos in the chorus, amplifying the sense of heartache and longing. Rodrigo's vocal performance is raw and vulnerable, effectively conveying the song's emotional weight.

Its emotional resonance and relatable storytelling makes it a standout debut for Olivia Rodrigo, and a universally loved song by Gen Z-ers and Millennials alike.

"drivers license" was her first music video for her album *SOUR*, directed by Matthew Dillon Cohen. Following the release of the video clip, thousands of TikTok users jumped in on the viral trend by recreating iconic scenes from the music video.

"1 step forward, 3 steps back"

"1 step forward, 3 steps back" is a song for all the Swifties out there. The melody interpolates Taylor Swift's song "New Year's Day," which adds a layer of familiarity and depth to the track, paying homage to one of Rodrigo's musical influences. The song is about someone in a relationship who is doing the most to keep it from crumbling. Olivia eloquently describes the rollercoaster of emotions brought on by the emotionally immature and unstable outbursts of a romantic partner. This song is simple and understated, with tender and nuanced storytelling, but it's her vocals that make this track an impactful one.

"deju vu"

After the release of her smash hit song "drivers license", Olivia Rodrigo was on a winning streak when she dropped her highly anticipated follow up single "deja vu". The song begins with a soft, almost haunting piano riff that gradually builds into a blend of dreamy synths, crisp percussion, and catchy, layered melodies that give the song an ethereal yet grounded feel. The song's lyrics revolve around the unsettling feeling of seeing an ex-partner replicate experiences and moments once shared together, with somebody new. The phrase "déjà vu" comes from the French language and describes a feeling that you have already experienced something that is actually happening for the first time.

"I thought it would be a cool play on words to use déjà vu as a metaphor for this very universal thing that happens when you break up with someone and they get with somebody else, and see them living the life that you lived with someone else," Rodrigo said about her second single, "It's just a super universal thing that I think happens to everyone that we just don't really talk about a ton...".

"deja vu" obviously got the music video treatment. The iconic clip, directed by Allie Avital, shows Olivia driving down the Californian coastline and wandering into a villa, only to find her ex-boyfriend's new girlfriend. She becomes completely fascinated with her ex's new love interest and starts to dress like her and replicate her hairstyles. Very soon her fixation turns obsessive, and Rodrigo is seen watching the new girl through a series of televisions. The director describes the narrative of the music video as a "mutual infatuation between the two girls, ultimately culminating in a merge of identities".

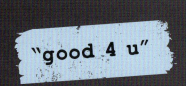 

"good 4 u"

"good 4 u" channels the energy and angst of early 2000s pop-punk, featuring gritty guitars, driving basslines, and a punchy drum beat. Olivia told American Songwriter in an interview about her writing process "we wanted to take an early 2000s pop-punk song and sort of twist it and find a way to make it 2021 ...I hope people are surprised". The song's lyrics are a biting commentary on the ease with which Rodrigo's ex has moved on to a new relationship, seemingly unaffected by their breakup. The sarcasm and bitterness in the lyrics highlight the dissonance between Rodrigo's internal struggle and her ex's outwardly smooth transition. Olivia's intense and fiery vocal performance really captures the feeling of rage one can feel following a breakup. She alternates between a softer, more controlled delivery in the verses and an explosive, impassioned belt in the chorus. This contrast really adds to the sense of catharsis exuding from this track. "good 4 u" is the perfect self-empowering anthem to add to a revenge playlist.

SOUR: THE ALBUM

The music video for "good 4 u" is yet another Petra Collins collaboration and is full of hidden references. When the music video opens, Olivia is shown in a buttoned-up, white collared shirt and red lipstick, very reminiscent of Lana Del Rey's look in the iconic cover art for her debut album, "*Born to Die*". Olivia is then seen sporting a cheerleader outfit in the same colour and style as Mandy Moore's outfit in The Princess Diaries. Throughout the clip, more references were made to movies like Jennifer's Body and Audition, but also to other musical artists like Taylor Swift's "Blank Space" and Kelly Clarkson's music video for "Since You've Been Gone".

Track seven could easily find a spot on Taylor Swift's albums *Fearless* or *Speak Now*. In this song, Olivia delves into the feelings of inadequacy and self-doubt that can often accompany a relationship where one partner feels they are never quite enough for the other. "enough for you" is a bittersweet and heart-wrenching song about literally drowning in so much love for someone, it compromises your identity and sense of self for them, only to have it unreciprocated.

Olivia alludes to all the things she did in order to please her ex, whether it was wearing more makeup or reading books to make herself seem smarter, in the hopes of being valued more. The acoustic arrangement of the track allows for Olivia's voice to shine and add an extra layer of vulnerability to an already personal song.

"happier"

The 8th track on her album arguably kickstarted Olivia's music career and subsequent widespread acclaim. She first met her longtime collaborator and co-writer, Dan Nigro, after he saw a video of her covering her song "happier" on Instagram. Dan was so blown away by the raw talent of the young musician that he sent her a DM message and the pair have remained inseparable ever since.

With the delicate piano melody and her heartfelt lyrics, "happier" has been a fan favourite since its release. In the song, Rodrigo articulates a hope that her ex finds happiness but not more than what they had together. She wants her old partner to be happy but ultimately she yearns for him to remember their time together as special, while grappling with the pain of being replaced.

The song beautifully and tenderly articulates the conflicting emotions of wanting the best for someone while still feeling the sting of being left behind.

Olivia Rodrigo ALL AMERICAN

"jealousy, jealousy"

Written by Olivia Rodrigo, Casey Smith, and her producer Dan Nigro, "jealousy, jealousy" delves into the toxic effects of social media and the comparison culture it perpetuates. Describing the song as "tongue-in-cheek and a little funny," Olivia revealed in an interview with NYLON that the track was actually about all the insecurities that come with growing up in the social media era — including the relentless pressure on users to maintain a flawless public image. "In this time period, I was super obsessed with social media," she shared. "I would look for things that would hurt my feelings all the time and compare myself to everyone".

This up tempo, alt rock song, serves as an edgy critique of the problematic digital landscape of the 21st century, something a lot of people can surely relate to... and now dance about.

"favorite crime"

The penultimate track on the album is a hauntingly beautiful song about the emotional turmoil of being in a relationship that was ultimately damaging. Olivia cleverly uses crime metaphors to describe the experience, calling herself a "willing accomplice", further illustrating her role in the destructive dynamics. In her Sour Composition book, where she details her songwriting process, she wrote on "favourite crime" "Dan & I wrote favourite crime sometime last summer, I think. I had 'know I loved you so bad I let you treat me like that' written in my notes app for a while & it sort of sparked the entire song".

The song captures the conflicting emotions of regret and longing, as she reflects on her actions and the pain they caused.

"hope ur ok"

The closing track "hope ur ok" is the perfect way to end the rollercoaster that is the *SOUR* album. The song stands out as a compassionate and heartfelt anthem of support and empathy, as Olivia tells the story of people from her past, who have faced adversity, and wishes them well. "hope ur ok" is the final track on *SOUR*, which would most likely represent the final stage of grief: acceptance. Olivia has mentioned that her favourite lyric she's ever written features in the song. She shared with Seventeen Magazine, "it's one of my faves. I think that song is really beautiful, too, as the last track on the album". This song is dedicated to all the outcasts out there and the lyrics serve as a gentle reminder of the impact kindness and understanding can have on individuals facing adversity.

SOUR: THE ALBUM

American Music Awards, November 2021, Los Angeles

Musical Controversy

Olivia Rodrigo faced criticism in the months following the release of her debut album, SOUR. These criticisms primarily revolved around alleged similarities between her songs and those of other artists.

"good 4 u" and Paramore's "Misery Business"

The most prominent criticism came from comparisons between Rodrigo's hit single "good 4 u" and Paramore's 2007 song "Misery Business". Fans were quick to draw similarities in the melody and overall pop-punk vibe, even going as far as creating mashups of the two songs. In response, Rodrigo and her team officially credited Paramore members Hayley Williams and Josh Farro as co-writers of "good 4 u."

"Deja Vu" and Taylor Swift's "Cruel Summer"

Her second single "deja vu" also came under fire for its striking likeness to Taylor Swift's hit song "Cruel Summer". Both tracks share thematic and lyrical similarities, with some listeners pointing out resemblances in melody and structure. Olivia has always been very vocal about Taylor being an influence on her music, but as a result she gave songwriting credits to Taylor Swift, Jack Antonoff and St. Vincent (who co-wrote "Cruel Summer") on "deja vu". This isn't the first instance that Olivia has used interpolations of Taylor Swift's work in her music. She interposed the piano melody from "New Year's day", off Taylor's Reputation album, in her song "1 step forward, 3 steps back". This created much less backlash as Swift and Antonoff were credited from the outset.

SOUR: THE ALBUM

"brutal" and Elvis Costello's "Pump It Up"

The last track to receive an onslaught of criticism was on "brutal" and its opening riff bearing a noticeable resemblance to Elvis Costello's song "Pump It Up". Elvis Costello has since come out and dismissed the allegations and even went to Twitter to defend similarities in music as part of the creative process. He tweeted, "This is fine by me... It's how rock and roll works. You take the broken pieces of another thrill and make a brand-new toy. That's what I did".

The *SOUR* claims sparked widespread discussion on the role of originality and song crediting in the music industry, but also highlighted the blurred lines between influence and imitation in art. Rodrigo has since responded to the criticism and told *Teen Vogue* that "nothing in music is ever new". She went onto say "what's so beautiful about music is that it can be so inspired by music that's come out in the past," admitting that she's had a "harder time learning" how to handle the business side of stardom.

Olivia is not the first nor the last artist to be scrutinised in this way. Ed Sheeran was embroiled in a highly mediatised lawsuit for his song "Thinking Out Loud", back in 2023. The family of the late singer Marvin Gaye accused Sheeran of copying the harmonic progressions, melodies and rhythmic elements from Gaye's iconic song "Let's Get It On", without permission.

Olivia at Le Zenith, Paris, 2022

SOUR Tour

The final instalment in the *SOUR* universe was, of course, Olivia Rodrigo's *SOUR* Tour. Olivia kicked off her first ever tour on April 5th, 2022, in Portland, Oregon, much to the excitement of her dedicated fan base.

The tour spanned several months and was comprised of 49 performances in major cities across North America and Europe. Fellow musicians Gracie Abrams, Holly Humberstone, and Baby Queen all served as opening acts for the highly anticipated concerts.

On December 10, tickets for the tour were made available to fans who were selected through the "Verified Fan" registration. The tickets sold out within minutes, a phenomenon many attributed to ticket scalpers, as some tickets appeared on resale sites for over $9,000 almost immediately. Olivia made headlines, yet again, for choosing to play smaller venues over arenas, with many media outlets citing her decision as a key reason why many fans couldn't secure tickets. Rodrigo defended her choice, telling the Los Angeles Times, "I don't think I should skip any steps," and assured fans, "there will be more tours in the future". Despite the initial criticism, the *SOUR* Tour quickly proved to be a remarkable success.

Each concert was a spectacle, combining stunning visuals, intimate acoustic sets, and energetic performances that left audiences in awe. And of course, some of Olivia's friends and peers made some surprise appearances.

SOUR TOUR, TORONTO 2022

Olivia Rodrigo ALL AMERICAN

Olivia at Glastonbury Festival, 2022

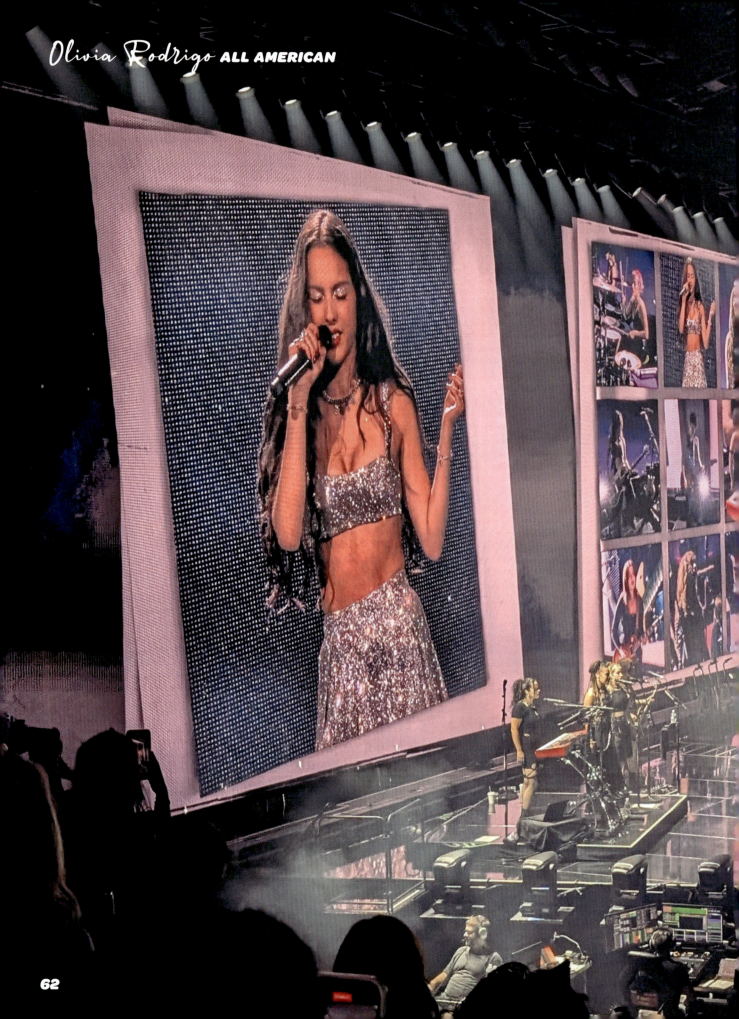

Olivia Rodrigo ALL AMERICAN

SOUR TOUR

Performing 'Ballad of a Homeschooled Girl,' in Atlanta, Georgia 2024

SOUR TOUR

Famous Friends

During the show in Vancouver, Conan Gray joined Rodrigo onstage to perform Katy Perry's "The One That Got Away".

Then in Olivia's first show in Toronto, she was joined onstage by Avril Lavigne to perform "Complicated".

During the first show in Los Angeles, Alanis Morissette joined Rodrigo onstage to perform her iconic song "You Oughta Know".

At Glastonbury Festival in Pilton, Lily Allen joined Rodrigo onstage to perform "Fuck You" in response to Roe V Wade being overturned in the United States.

During the first show in London, Natalie Imbruglia joined Rodrigo onstage to perform "Torn".

Lily Allen and Olivia perform on the Other Stage at Glastonbury Festival, 2022

Olivia Rodrigo ALL AMERICAN

The visual elements of the *SOUR Tour* were as striking as the performances themselves. The stage design was a vibrant reflection of the album's aesthetic, featuring a mix of pastel colours, grungy textures, and dynamic lighting. Large video screens displayed evocative imagery that complemented the themes of each song, enhancing the overall concert experience.

Olivia's fashion choices also played a significant role in the tour's visual impact. She donned a variety of outfits that ranged from edgy and rebellious to soft and nostalgic, mirroring the emotional spectrum of her music. Each ensemble added a layer of storytelling, making the performances not just auditory but also visual feasts.

The biggest highlight from Olivia's *SOUR Tour* was the genuine connection she shared with her fans. Throughout the concerts, Rodrigo took time to interact with the audience, sharing personal anecdotes and expressing her gratitude for their support. This authenticity resonated deeply, creating a sense of community and shared experience among concertgoers.

She ended her tour in London, and with a final farewell to the crowd, she disappeared into a sea of purple confetti. It was the perfect send-off to both the night and the tour as a whole.

Rodrigo proved that she is not just a fleeting pop sensation but a lasting force in the music industry. The *SOUR Tour* cemented her as a bona fide pop superstar, as fans continue to revel in the memories of the experience. Everyone is at the edge of their seats wondering what will come next from the young new artist.

Olivia Rodrigo Billboard on Sunset Blvd, Los Angeles, 2022

driving home 2 u

"driving home 2 u" is not just a standard music documentary; it's a road trip through the emotional and physical landscapes that shaped *SOUR*. The film, directed by Stacey Lee, follows Olivia as she retraces the journey from Salt Lake City to Los Angeles, a trip she made frequently during the creation of her album.

The documentary provides a rare glimpse into the behind-the-scenes moments that fans rarely get to see. From late-night studio sessions to candid conversations with collaborators, "driving home 2 u" captures the highs and lows of the creative process.

Rodrigo also reflects on her rapid rise to fame after the release of her smash single "drivers license" and the personal experiences that inspired her debut album. She speaks candidly about heartbreak, self-discovery, and the pressures of sudden stardom.

The film's cinematography captures the vast, picturesque landscapes of the American West, creating a visually stunning backdrop for the young popstar's story. The juxtaposition of expansive scenery with the intimate, personal moments of songwriting and introspection mirrors the themes found in *SOUR*. "driving home 2 u" is the perfect ending to an incredible chapter in Olivia Rodrigo's career.

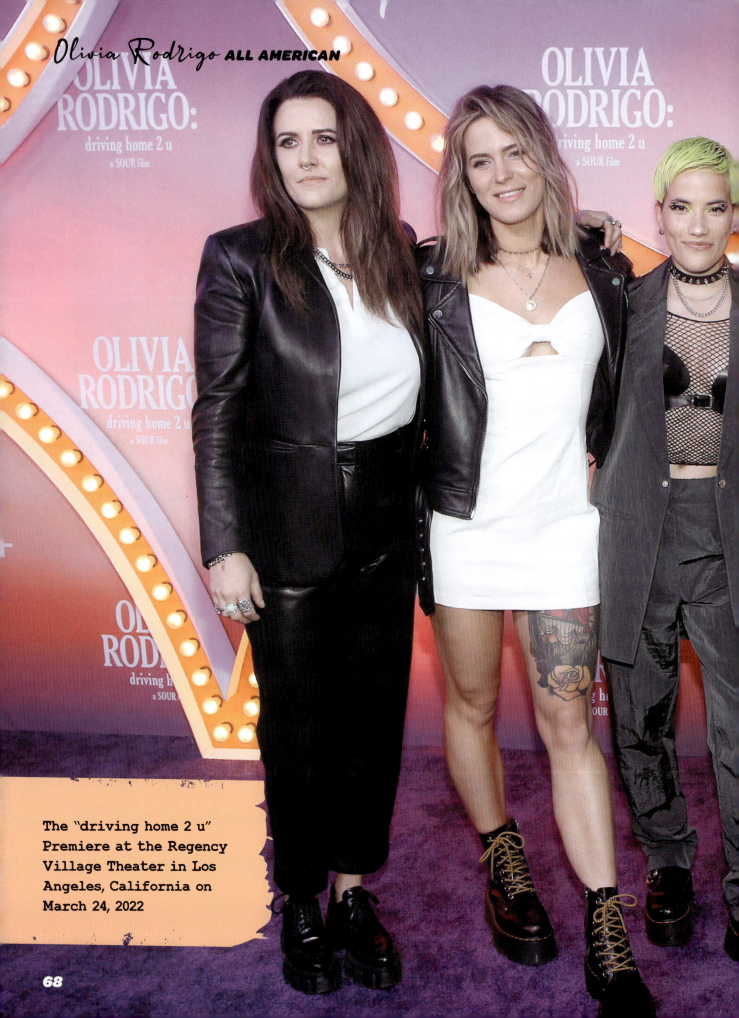

Olivia Rodrigo **ALL AMERICAN**

The "driving home 2 u" Premiere at the Regency Village Theater in Los Angeles, California on March 24, 2022

Life after Sour

After the monumental success of her debut album "*SOUR*," Olivia Rodrigo could have easily taken a well-deserved break. However, instead of resting on her laurels, she chose to dive deeper into her craft, channelling her energy and creativity into new projects and expanding her brand.

Embracing her newfound fame, Olivia continued to evolve as an artist, exploring different musical styles and themes in her subsequent work. She also ventured into various collaborations, leveraging her platform to support causes close to her heart.

Olivia greeting fans at the NBC Today Show, New York City, 2023

LIFE AFTER SOUR

71

Olivia Rodrigo ALL AMERICAN
Brand Partnerships

CASETiFY

Olivia Rodrigo expanded her creative horizons through her dynamic partnership with CASETiFY, the global tech accessory brand known for its fashionable and functional phone cases. This collaboration, which was announced in 2022, merges Rodrigo's distinctive artistic style with CASETiFY's commitment to quality, resulting in a collection that resonates with Olivia Rodrigo fans and tech enthusiasts alike.

The Olivia Rodrigo x CASETiFY collection features a range of customizable phone cases and accessories that reflect the youthful, edgy, and vibrant aesthetic of Olivia's brand. The "hardened hearts" designs incorporate elements from her hit album *SOUR*, including lyrics, motifs, and colour schemes that fans will instantly recognize.

In addition to the cute designs, Olivia's collection uses recycled materials to make the phone cases. CASETiFY also created the Re/CASETiFY program, allowing customers to send in old phone cases to be recycled, reducing waste and promoting a circular economy. This initiative aligns with Rodrigo's advocacy for environmental sustainability, making the collaboration not only stylish but also socially responsible.

Glossier

In Glossier's new collaboration with Olivia Rodrigo, the signature baby pink is swapped out for lavender, marking the beauty brand's first-ever partnership with a celebrity since its founding in 2014. The collaboration includes a range of items such as lip glosses, cheek tints, and eyeshadows, each designed to be versatile and easy to use, aligning with Glossier's "skin first, makeup second" philosophy. "Less is more with skin care and makeup a lot of the time, and I've found when I keep things simple I feel the best too," Rodrigo told Vogue, when discussing her line of products.

In keeping with the campaign's aim to promote and embrace the natural beauty of the user, all images showcasing the products are unedited shots of Olivia.

Both Olivia Rodrigo and Glossier share a commitment to sustainability and inclusivity. The collection includes eco-friendly packaging options and cruelty-free formulations, reflecting their dedication to environmentally conscious practices. Additionally, the products are designed to be inclusive, with shades and formulas that cater to a diverse range of skin tones and types.

The packaging, featuring pastel hues and playful designs, draws inspiration from Rodrigo's *"SOUR"* album aesthetics, creating a cohesive visual identity that resonates with her fans. The names of the products also nod to her music, with clever references that add a personal touch to the collection.

Despite her rapid rise to fame, Olivia has demonstrated a profound commitment to giving back and making a positive impact on society.

Philanthropy

"Spicy Pisces"

In February 2021, Olivia Rodrigo launched her merchandise line, "Spicy Pisces T-shirts," on her website. All proceeds from the sales were donated to She's the First (STF), a non-governmental organization dedicated to breaking the cycle of poverty by educating and empowering young girls across the globe. Founded in 2009 by Tammy Tibbetts and Christen Brandt, the organization focuses on providing scholarships and fostering leadership development for girls in low-income countries, ensuring they are the first in their families to graduate from high school.

The "Spicy Pisces" t-shirts, inspired by Rodrigo's own zodiac sign, blend her love for astrology with her unique sense of style as well as her commitment to philanthropy. As a Pisces, Olivia is known for her creativity, empathy, and emotional depth—traits that resonate deeply in her music. These t-shirts reflect not just her star sign but also the fiery, passionate side of her personality, encapsulating the dual nature of being a Pisces... and they are for an amazing cause so what's not to love?

Olivia Rodrigo ALL AMERICAN

LIFE AFTER SOUR

> President Joe Biden and Olivia Rodrigo record a video address in the Oval Office, 2021

In July 2021, Olivia Rodrigo visited the White House to support the Biden administration's efforts to promote COVID-19 vaccinations among young people. The 18-year-old pop star (at the time) participated in a series of events aimed at encouraging vaccination, including a meeting with President Joe Biden and Dr. Anthony Fauci. She also delivered a speech in the White House briefing room, expressing her honour and humility at being able to contribute to such an important cause. She emphasized the importance of youth vaccinations and encouraged conversations among friends and family to promote vaccine uptake saying, "It's so important to get vaccinated, even if you're young and healthy and not at risk. Vaccines help everyone. Just because you're not particularly at risk doesn't mean that people close to you aren't".

During her visit, Rodrigo filmed several videos aimed at spreading awareness about the vaccine. She also shared a lighthearted moment with President Biden, who gifted her a pair of his signature aviator Ray-Bans, presidential M&Ms, and a shoehorn.

Olivia Rodrigo ALL AMERICAN

"Fuck You"

The "drivers license" singer has also long been a champion of reproductive rights, with her notably taking a stand against the US Supreme Court's decision to overturn Roe v. Wade at the 2022 Glastonbury festival.

During her set, Olivia Rodrigo delivered a powerful and politically charged performance that left an indelible mark on the audience. Rodrigo, known for her raw and emotional music, heavily criticized the US Supreme Court's recent decision to overturn Roe v. Wade, a landmark ruling that had protected women's reproductive rights for nearly five decades.

She surprised all the festival-goers by inviting British singer Lily Allen to join her onstage. Together, they performed Allen's 2009 hit "Fuck You," a song known for its explicit criticism of oppressive authority figures. The choice of song and the context of the performance resonated deeply with the crowd, turning it into a moment of solidarity and defiance.

Before launching into the song, Olivia addressed the audience with a heartfelt and impassioned speech. "I'm devastated and terrified. So many women and so many girls are going to die because of this. I wanted to dedicate this next song to the five members of the Supreme Court who have showed us that at the end of the day, they truly don't give a sh*t about freedom. The song is for the Justices Samuel Alito, Clarence Thomas, Neil Gorsuch, Amy Coney Barrett, Brett Kavanaugh. We hate you! We hate you."

LIFE AFTER SOUR

"Can't Catch Me Now" is a song by American singer-songwriter Olivia Rodrigo from the soundtrack of "The Hunger Games: The Ballad of Songbirds & Snakes" (2023). Rodrigo co-wrote the song with its producer, Dan Nigro. Geffen Records released "Can't Catch Me Now" as the soundtrack album's second single on November 3, 2023. The song won the Hollywood Music in Media Award for Best Original Song in a Sci-Fi, Fantasy, or Horror Film at the 2023 ceremony.

"I'm such a big fan of all things Hunger Games, and I love the soundtracks", Olivia said about her contribution to the franchise, "so when they asked if I wanted to write it, I was so stoked and I went in and watched the movie, and was really inspired by the main character, Lucy Gray".

The Ballad of Songbirds & Snakes follows a young Coriolanus Snow (Tom Blyth) as he mentors District 12 tribute and songstress Lucy Gray Baird (Rachel Zegler).

"Can't Catch Me Now" was also shortlisted for the "Best Original Song" category at the 96th Academy Awards but did not make it to the final nominees.

Despite Olivia's busy work schedule, she still makes time to date. Balancing her rapidly growing career with her personal life, Olivia ensures that she carves out moments for relationships amidst her demanding commitments. Whether she's touring, recording new music, or engaging in various projects, she prioritizes maintaining a semblance of normalcy by nurturing her personal connections.

Olivia Rodrigo **ALL AMERICAN**

LIFE AFTER SOUR

Olivia Rodrigo accepting Songwriter of the Year at Variety's Hitmakers Brunch, Los Angeles 2021

i'm so obsessed with my ex(s)

Adam Faze
(June 2021- January 2022)

A month after Olivia Rodrigo released her record-smashing debut album *SOUR*, E! News reported that the then-18-year-old singer was dating someone new, then-24-year-old producer Adam Faze. Like Rodrigo, Faze is no stranger to the entertainment industry. In addition to directing Goody Grace's "Nothing Good" music video, he also works as a producer in film and TV, but before embarking on his career as a producer, Faze was a writer for Forbes. He later explained on Twitter that his passion was always "making movies" and has since made the switch in careers.

Olivia attended the July 2021 premiere of Space Jam: A New Legacy with Adam as her plus-one, sparking dating rumours between the two.

Two weeks later, paparazzi captured the couple kissing on the streets of Los Angeles. Despite this public display, they kept their relationship relatively private during the six months they were together.

In January 2022, fans speculated about their breakup when Olivia unfollowed Adam on Instagram, although he was still following her at the time. The breakup was confirmed in February by People, with an insider noting, "They've been over for a bit now."

LIFE AFTER SOUR

Zack Bia
(February - August 2022)

Zack Bia is a prominent figure in the entertainment industry, known for his roles as a DJ, music executive, and entrepreneur. He first gained attention in the Los Angeles nightlife scene, where he became a well-known promoter and socialite. Bia also co-founded Field Trip Recordings, a music label that aims to support and promote emerging artists.

The 28-year-old DJ, whose full name is Zack Bialobos, has mingled with many famous personalities over the years. In addition to being friends with stars, Bia has also been romantically connected to some big names. Before sparking romance rumours with Olivia Rodrigo, he dated singer Madison Beer for a year before splitting in 2019.

He made headlines in 2022 when he was spotted with Olivia Rodrigo. During Olivia's *SOUR* Tour, the pair were seen together in New York City in April 2022, just before her concert at Radio City Music Hall.

Their romance was later confirmed by People in June, with a source revealing, "They've been dating since the Super Bowl. They really like each other." However, their relationship eventually ended, with multiple outlets reporting their breakup in August 2022.

ZACK BIA

Olivia Rodrigo ALL AMERICAN

37th Annual Rock & Roll Hall of Fame Induction Ceremony, 2022

LIFE AFTER SOUR

Olivia cheers at the USC vs. UCLA game, Los Angeles, 2023

LIFE AFTER SOUR

GUTS: the album

Olivia Rodrigo broke the second album curse with the release of her sophomore record *GUTS*.

GUTS marks a bold and introspective continuation of her musical journey following the success of her debut album, *SOUR*. Released in 2023, *GUTS* delves deeper into themes of self-discovery, emotional growth, and the complexities of young adulthood. The album showcases Olivia's maturation as both a songwriter and a vocalist, with lyrics that are raw, honest, and deeply personal.

Olivia told the BBC it was a "happier" and "more playful" record than her debut, with a rockier sound inspired by her forthcoming tour. "It's such a cathartic experience to sing songs like that in a crowd". Released in September, *GUTS* quickly topped the UK and US charts, and has been nominated for six Grammy Awards, including Album of The Year.

Rolling Stone magazine called it "another instant classic", while AllMusic called Rodrigo an "artist with plenty of things to say, and the confidence and eloquence to say them her way".

While her debut was largely written about one disastrous relationship, *GUTS* finds her discussing fame, pain, questionable hook-ups, self-sabotage, and stumbling into adulthood.

Breaking Records

In the United States, *GUTS* debuted at number one on Billboard 200 chart, becoming Olivia's second album to top the chart. The record also accumulated a total of 199.59 million on-demand streams, with all 12 tracks charting in the top 40 of the Hot 100, including a return to the number-one spot for her lead single 'vampire.'

GUTS was nominated 6 times for a Grammy, including for Best Album of The Year and Best Pop Vocal Album. It also won Album of The Year at the 2024 People's Choice Awards and the iHeartRadio Music Awards, as well as a load more accolades.

On May 21, 2023, the second anniversary of *SOUR*, Olivia shared a 2-second snippet of a song (which would later be confirmed to be "bad Idea right?") on the upcoming album via Instagram. Later, on the 27th of May, Rodrigo shared a mirror selfie on Instagram. Eagle eyed viewers quickly spotted the date "June 30th, 2023", circled with a heart on the singer's calendar. On the 13th June, Olivia finally announced the album's lead single, "vampire" would be released at the end of the month and eventually become an instant hit.

OLIVIA'S ACCEPTANCE SPEECH, IHEARTMUSIC AWARD, 2024

GUTS: THE ALBUM

Stellar Singles

"vampire" topped the charts in Australia, Canada, Ireland, Israel, Japan, New Zealand, the United Kingdom, and the United States, becoming Rodrigo's third chart-topping single in all eight countries.

It received the nominations for Record of the Year, Song of the Year and Best Pop Solo Performance at the 66th Annual Grammy Awards. Its music video won an MTV Video Music Award for Best Editing during the 2023 ceremony.

Discussing the name Guts, and how she came up with it, in an Apple Music interview, Olivia said: "I've had it for a long time. I had it actually when I was making *SOUR*. I'm like, 'I want the next one to be Guts'. I like had it in my head, four letters, all caps, just like Sour, I love it."

Olivia then explained what it means to her. She added: "I just think it's an interesting word. People use it in so many interesting contexts, like 'Spill your guts'. 'Hate your guts'. It means bravery, but it also means intuition, like listen to your gut. I just think it's all of these things that coincidentally were things that I've really been thinking about in this chapter".

Her album cover for her record *GUTS* includes her iconic purple backdrop, although this time a slightly darker shade than the one used on *SOUR*, perhaps signifying a more mature record than her previous debut album.

Rodrigo is seen sporting a lacy black dress and red lipstick lying on a purple backdrop, wearing four rings on her fingers that spell out the project's title.

"I made the bulk of this album during my 19th year on this earth," the former Disney actress said in a statement at the time of the album announcement.

"A year that, for me, was filled with lots of confusion, mistakes, awkwardness & good old fashioned teen angst".

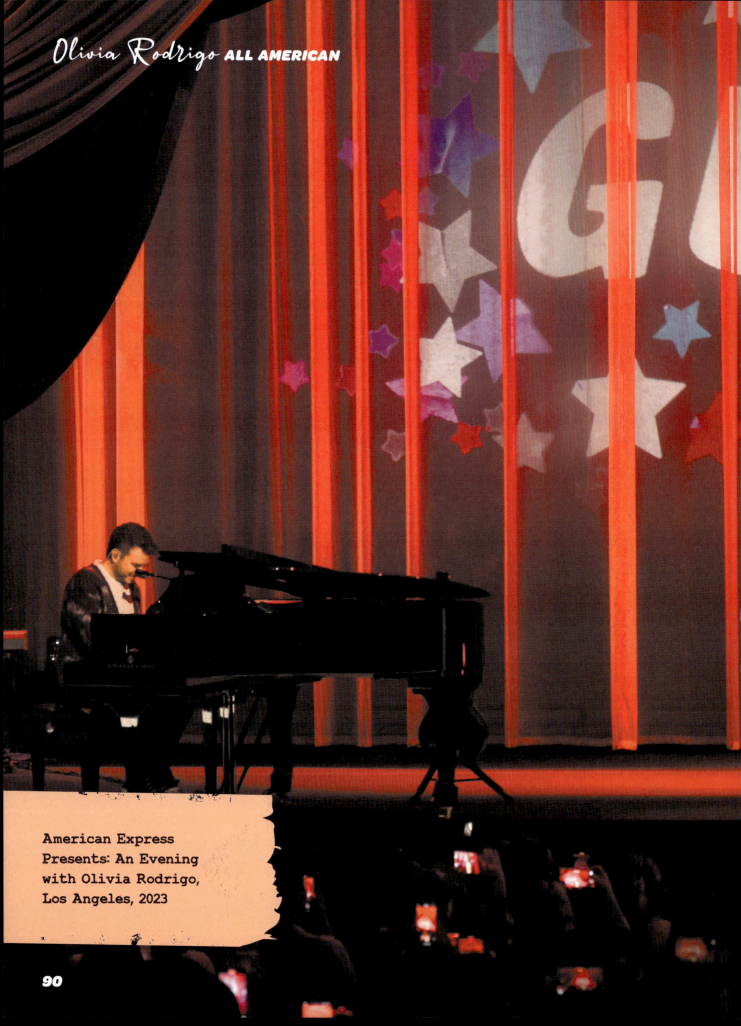

American Express Presents: An Evening with Olivia Rodrigo, Los Angeles, 2023

GUTS: THE ALBUM

Olivia takes the stage to perform 'Vampire' at the 66th Annual Grammy Awards, Los Angeles 2024

GUTS: THE ALBUM

Tracklist

all-american b****

bad idea right?

vampire

lacy

ballad of a homeschooled girl

making the bed

logical

get him back!

love is embarrassing

the grudge

pretty isn't pretty

teenage dream

Olivia Rodrigo ALL AMERICAN
Track by Track Analysis

"all-american b****"

"all-american b****" is the perfect opening track for this album. The young singer really let her vocal skills shine in this song, kicking off the album with a lot of angst, completely setting the tone for the rest of the project. The track begins with a gentle strumming of the guitar, which quickly escalates into an explosive burst of punk energy with overdrive guitar, only to switch back unexpectedly. The song delves into themes of identity, societal expectations, and the pressures to conform. Rodrigo's lyrics are sharp and incisive, capturing the frustration and disillusionment of trying to live up to an idealized image of perfection. The transitions from the mellow verses to the more intense chorus are seamless, reflecting the internal conflict and emotional turbulence described in the lyrics.

In an interview with Apple Music, Olivia shared her affection for the song, saying, "I really love the song. It's one of my favourite songs I've ever written. I really love the lyrics and I think it expresses something I've been trying to convey since I was 15 years old—this repressed anger and confusion, or the feeling of being put into a box as a girl." Initially starting as a piano piece, the song eventually evolved into an "intense rock song." Rodrigo mentioned that the title was inspired by an essay by Joan Didion, specifically the titular essay in Slouching Towards Bethlehem.

Right off the bat, Olivia showcases her evolving artistry while still maintaining the authenticity and lyrical prowess that made her a breakout star... from the very first notes of "all-american b****", her sophomore album promises to be another gem.

"bad idea right?"

Olivia Rodrigo is a masterful chronicler of pivotal "firsts": first love, first heartbreak, etc... On the second single from her second album, GUTS, she explores an equally significant moment in any young person's life: the first backslide. Wry and fast-paced, Olivia injects playful comedy into her music, along with the seed of wounded irony reminiscent of her track "brutal" from her debut album SOUR. "bad idea right?" is an upbeat track that narrates Rodrigo's internal conflict about reconnecting with her ex-boyfriend after a night out with friends. The song vividly captures her thought process, showcasing a dynamic, back-and-forth argument with herself as she weighs the pros and cons of her decision. "'bad idea right?' started with us making a joke song about me hooking up with an ex-boyfriend, but then we realized we were actually onto something," Olivia said in a statement about the track. "We were throwing the weirdest things at the wall — in one of the choruses there's a part that sounds like an instrument in the background, but it's me gradually screaming louder and louder".

"bad idea right?" is the second single and second music video from Rodrigo's sophomore album and yet another Petra Collins collaboration. The fuzzy video, reminiscent of an "early '90s B-movie horror-comedy", opens at a house party where Olivia and her real-life best friends Tate McRae, Iris Apatow, and Madison Hu are gathered in the bathroom. As she wanders through the party, random attendees affirm that it's a "bad idea, right?". But Rodrigo brushes them off, telling herself, "Fuck it, it's fine." She then embarks on a journey to her ex's place, hitchhiking on the back of a truck in the rain and getting splashed by a slushie on public transit until she finally arrives.

The song is highly theorized to be about Joshua Bassett because of hints in the music video with the "ex," who plays the guitar and lives in apartment 22, coincidentally the date of Joshua Bassett's birthday (December 22, 2002). Additionally, since the pair were seen smiling and laughing together at the season 3 premier of High School Musical: The Musical: The Series, many fans have been hoping for a rekindling between the two former flames.

"vampire"

After a two-year break, Olivia Rodrigo came back in full swing in 2023 with the release of her first single "vampire" off her new album, GUTS.

Described vaguely by Rodrigo as a song that "reflects the pent-up anger that you have for a situation," the track surges in strength over its four-minute run time. What begins as a piano-backed ballad slowly crescendoes in volume, until the singer is belting at her ex at the top of her lungs over a thumping, synth-driven release.

"Writing this song helped me sort through lots of feelings of regret, anger, and heartache," she said of the track on social media. "It's one of my favorite songs on the album and it felt very cathartic to finish. I'm so happy it's in your hands now and I hope it helps u deal with any bloodsuckers in your life."

Olivia Rodrigo's lyrical talent really shines in "vampire." The song addresses the pain of being used and deceived by someone she trusted, using the metaphor of a vampire to illustrate the draining and predatory nature of the relationship. The rock opera track alludes to an age gap in the relationship, which would make sense to anyone who has followed Olivia's dating life over the past few years. The former Disney actress has been linked to two significantly older

Olivia Rodrigo ALL AMERICAN

men in the past: producer Adam Faze, whom she reportedly dated for about six months when she was 18, and DJ Zack Bia, whom she dated around the age of 19. The vampire metaphor is particularly apt as typically vampires look as if they never age, but, in reality, are very old in terms of years.

Of course, the lead single of GUTS would get the music video treatment. The "vampire" music video, directed by Petra Collins, opens with a stark, ethereal scene, featuring Rodrigo bathed in moonlight against a desolate, forested backdrop. Collins' direction leans heavily into gothic and surrealist imagery, giving off very *Twilight* vibes indeed.

"lacy"

In 2022, while crafting her album GUTS, Olivia attended a poetry class at the University of Southern California, and ended up repurposing one of her homework pieces into the song that would later be known as "lacy".

The lyrics of "lacy" delve into complex emotions, particularly the feelings of envy and admiration that can arise in relationships. Rodrigo sings about Lacy, a seemingly perfect figure who embodies qualities that the narrator feels she lacks. Olivia perfectly juxtaposes the feelings of admiration and jealousy— recognizing someone's beauty and grace while feeling inadequate in comparison. The lyrics in this track are very reminiscent of Dolly Parton's 1973 hit, "Jolene", with both songs sharing themes of admiration turned obsessive.

PERFORMING AT THE O2

There is a debate about the subject of this song. Some fans believe the track to be about Madison Beer, who had previously dated Zack Bia, or Sabrina Carpenter, who famously, dated Joshua Bassett after Olivia. Another theory is that "lacy" could be about a romantic attraction Olivia had to a woman, due to the LGBT implications of the lyrics, though the singer has never confirmed nor denied rumours about her sexuality.

lacy keeps the "finger-picked folk-pop [sound] that popped up a few times on *SOUR*" while highlighting Rodrigo's more sophisticated storytelling.

GUTS: THE ALBUM

"ballad of a homeschooled girl"

The fifth track of the album delves into the unique challenges and feelings of isolation that can come with being homeschooled. Rodrigo opens up about her personal experiences, addressing themes of social anxiety, self-doubt, and the struggle to fit in. She perfectly captures the awkwardness and confusion of navigating social situations as a homeschooled teenager. This song is funny and honest as Olivia describes all the small social mistakes she has made in public settings, and laments on how she feels her every move will ultimately lead to "social suicide." The introspective lyrics nicely contrast the lively pop-punk arrangement and vibrant tone, adding to the humoristic aspect of the song.

"making the bed"

The song's title refers to the expression "You made your bed, now lie in it", a comment someone may receive after complaining about the consequences of their actions. Rodrigo uses the metaphor of "making the bed" to symbolize the routine of maintaining appearances and the exhaustion that comes with it. Rodrigo laments her decisions and acknowledges her own mistakes, demonstrating self-awareness by admitting she's "making the bed" herself.

"making the bed" features a moody, atmospheric arrangement that sets a contemplative tone from the outset, while showcasing her hauntingly beautiful lyrics and vocal performance. This track is a standout from her sophomore album, as it really demonstrated the growth of the young singer.

"logical"

"logical" is a devastating song in the best possible way. It's exactly what Olivia Rodrigo does best: take a complicated emotion and turn it into a beautifully simple and relatable piece of music. The lyrics of "logical" delve into the paradoxes and contradictions inherent in love and relationships. Rodrigo sings about the struggle between logic and emotion, capturing the confusion and pain of being in a situation where love defies reason. The subject of Olivia's song hits where it hurts, using factors like her age and naivety against her, similar to what Taylor Swift writes about in "All Too Well".

Olivia makes numerous references to her song "vampire", leading fans to speculate that the subject of the song is none other than Zack Bia.

"get him back!"

"get him back!" riffs on the dual interpretation of those same words: 'get him back' as in restore the relationship, and 'get him back' as in procure revenge. This clever double entendre really accentuates the confused feelings of wanting to forget an ex but not wanting to be forgotten by them. Olivia spoke with Zane Lowe about "get him back!" in an interview for Apple Music, saying "I had such a desire to live and experience things and make mistakes and grow after SOUR came out, I kind of felt this pressure to be this girl that I thought everyone expected me to be. I think because of that pressure, maybe I did things that maybe I shouldn't have—dated people that I shouldn't have".

The song is anchored by a punchy drumbeat and gritty guitar riffs, creating a sound that is both energetic and edgy, yet another perfect breakup anthem to dance to.

The music video for "get him back!" is characterized by its vibrant and dynamic visual style. The use of bold colors, quick cuts, and playful imagery creates an engaging and high-energy atmosphere that mirrors the song's upbeat tempo. Directed by Jack Begert, the video's visual style is reminiscent of early 2000s pop-punk aesthetics, with a modern twist. The clip was also entirely filmed on an iPhone 15 Pro Max, and was released on September 12, 2023, shortly after the announcement of the device.

Additionally, the song was featured in the first trailer for the 2024 film adaptation of the 2017 musical Mean Girls and in the video game Fortnite Festival.

"love is embarrassing"

Self-reflection is a big theme on her most recent album GUTS, and "love is embarrassing" is no different. Rodrigo reflects on past relationships and the mistakes she made, using humour and self-deprecation to convey her experiences. The lyrics of "love is embarrassing" are direct and relatable, capturing the awkwardness and humiliation that often accompany young love. She dives deep into those cringe-worthy moments when she realized that she put her heart out on the line for someone who wasn't worth it, and more importantly, wasn't interested. Throughout the song, Olivia Rodrigo lays bare her regrets, admitting to waiting by the phone for calls that never echoed and getting tangled up with a person she now labels as a loser who's not worth mentioning.

The production is polished yet maintains a sense of rawness that aligns with the song's honest and confessional tone. The fast tempo of this song coincides with the heart-racing feeling of being embarrassed and the quickness of the relationship Rodrigo is describing, as well as creates a contrast with the song's introspective lyrics, making it a compelling and engaging listen.

"the grudge"

Olivia Rodrigo is no stranger to the feelings of betrayal. In her previous album, SOUR, she even dedicated an entire track to singing about how an ex-boyfriend had once betrayed her, in her hit song "traitor". For her sophomore album, GUTS, little has changed as she still uses her painful life experiences as fodder for her music, although now the emotions feel a little more grown up and heartbreaking. GUTS contains quite a few tearjerkers, however, "the grudge" seems to be ripped straight out of Olivia's diary. This deeply personal song delves into the lingering confusion, pain and bitterness of betrayal that often follows the end of a tumultuous relationship. Rodrigo sings about the difficulty of letting go of a grudge, capturing the internal struggle between wanting to move on but being unable to forgive. Adding to her pain, the person who wronged her doesn't seem to acknowledge any wrongdoing, denying her any apology for the hurt inflicted. The young singer is just left with a heap of unanswered questions and no way of getting the closure she so desperately craves.

"the grudge" features a sombre, melancholic arrangement that sets a reflective tone from the outset. The song opens with a delicate piano melody which gradually builds in intensity, adding layers of depth and emotion without overshadowing Rodrigo's vocal performance, the true star of the show.

Following the release of the song, fans have speculated about its inspiration. Is it the "bloodsucker" from "vampire," the "master manipulator" from "logical," or the not-six-foot-two ex from "get him back!"? As different theories started the swirl on social media, one main speculation was that the subject of the song is none other than pop peer Taylor Swift.

When Olivia Rodrigo burst onto the music scene with her debut single "drivers license" in January 2021, she quickly gained attention from music enthusiasts and industry veterans alike. Among her early supporters was Taylor Swift. Rodrigo openly expressed her admiration for Swift, citing her as a major inspiration. This mutual respect seemed to blossom into a genuine friendship, with both singers posting messages of solidarity to each other on social media.

However, speculation about tension between Olivia and Taylor arose after Rodrigo had to hand over 50 percent of the royalties of her song "deja vu" to Swift due to its similarities with "Cruel Summer." Despite the quiet handling of these credit disputes, the once-budding public friendship between the two pop icons appeared to sour.

Now, two years later, fans are convinced that Rodrigo's song "the grudge" reflects her feelings about being let down by someone she once idolized.

There were also rumours going around claiming that Olivia's song "vampire" is also about Swift. She quickly shut down those theories and told The Guardian "I mean, I never want to say who any of my songs are about. I've never done that before in my career and probably won't. I think it's better to not pigeonhole a song to being about this one thing." She added, "I was very surprised when people thought that".

Olivia Rodrigo ALL AMERICAN

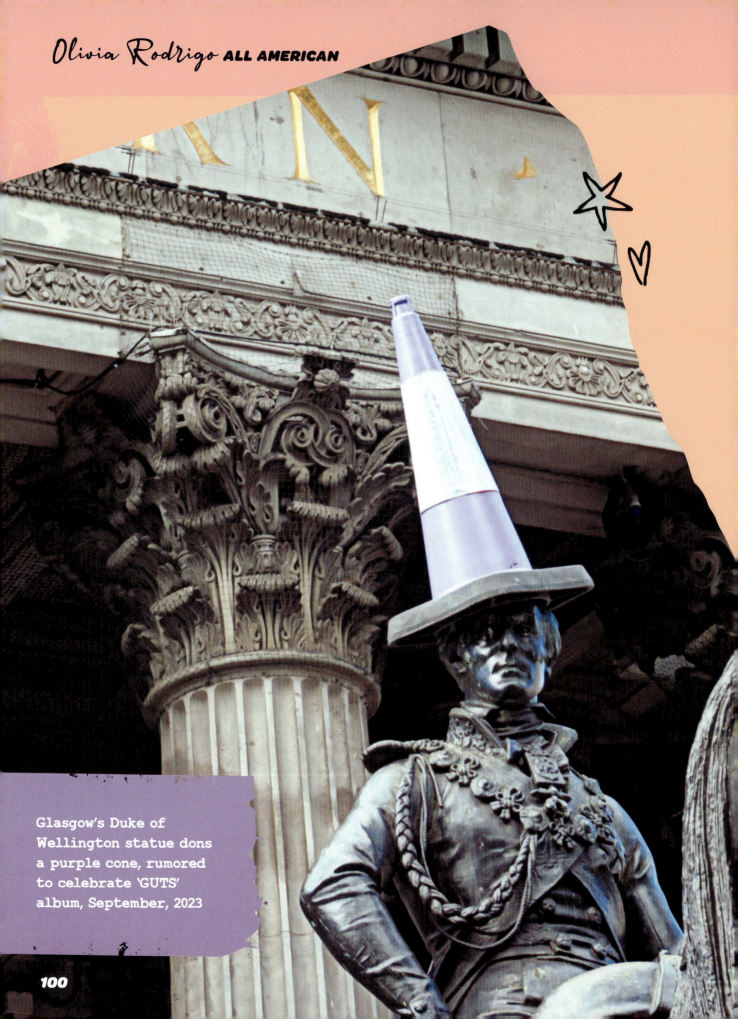

Glasgow's Duke of Wellington statue dons a purple cone, rumored to celebrate 'GUTS' album, September, 2023

GUTS: THE ALBUM

"pretty isn't pretty"

Although most of Rodrigo's songs deal with the affairs of the heart, in "pretty isn't pretty" the young popstar explores her feelings of inadequacy and the pressures she feels to conform to societal beauty standards, as well as the internal conflict it creates. Rodrigo sings about the relentless pursuit of physical perfection and the realization that achieving these standards doesn't lead to true happiness but rather highlights the futility and frustration of this pursuit.

Similar to "all-american b****" and "lacy," Rodrigo details the many things she feels she should do in order to conform to these standards. The lyrics of "pretty isn't pretty" echo the sentiments of her debut album track "jealousy, jealousy." However, in this song, Olivia arrives at the realization that these standards are inherently unfair and will always make her feel less than others due to how society views women's bodies and appearances.

This track is deeply vulnerable yet highly relatable, especially in a time where social media is as prevalent as it is today.

"teenage dream"

If we take a trip down memory lane and look at Olivia's debut album SOUR, the phrase "teenage dream" came up in her music before. In SOUR's opening track "brutal," one of the most iconic lines includes those words. Olivia Rodrigo's "teenage dream" is a poignant reflection on the pressures and fears of growing up, especially as a young woman in the public eye. The song delves into the complexities of transitioning from adolescence to adulthood, grappling with the expectations placed on young people, and the nostalgia for simpler times. Rodrigo's introspective lyrics question the inevitability of maturity and the loss of innocence that accompanies it, offering a heartfelt exploration of the bittersweet emotions of growing up.

When SOUR was released, Olivia was 18 years old, and then 20 for the release of GUTS. "teenage dream" basically sums up her journey from adolescence to early adulthood. She's essentially saying, "I'm sorry that I couldn't always be your teenage dream," as she reflects on the years she's grown since her debut album, and what it means to bid that era of her life goodbye.

GUTS: THE ALBUM

Olivia Rodrigo during the opening night of the GUTS Tour, Palm Springs, California 2024

Guts Spilled

On March 22nd, 2024, Olivia Rodrigo delighted fans worldwide with the release of *GUTS Spilled*, the deluxe edition of her critically acclaimed second studio album *GUTS*.

The original GUTS album, released in September 2023, solidified Olivia's position as a pop powerhouse, building on the success of her debut album *SOUR*. With its raw emotion, candid storytelling, and blend of pop-punk and indie-rock influences, her sophomore album explored all the complexities that come with growing up. With *GUTS Spilled*, Rodrigo expands on these themes, diving even deeper into her personal experiences and artistic vision. The deluxe edition features five brand new tracks including the fan favourite song "obsessed".

Olivia taking over the billboard along Wilshire Blvd, Los Angeles 2024

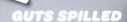

Olivia Rodrigo **ALL AMERICAN**

Track by Track Analysis

"obsessed"

When she initially released her second studio album *GUTS*, the song was included exclusively on special editions of the CD and vinyl, meaning only a select group of fans had the chance to hear it. However, it didn't take long for the song to leak online and go viral on TikTok, prompting fans to beg for its release on streaming platforms. Rodrigo has now answered their prayers.

During her worldwide tour, the 21-year-old singer further teased her audience by performing "obsessed" live, which only heightened the anticipation for its official release.

The demand for its official release was overwhelming, and Rodrigo delivered, much to the delight of her dedicated fanbase.

At its core, "obsessed" explores the consuming nature of infatuation. The lyrics depict a narrative of someone who is deeply fixated on another person to the point where it borders on unhealthy obsession. Rodrigo's storytelling prowess shines as she details the all-encompassing thoughts and actions that accompany such a state. "obsessed" is a perfect example of what Olivia does best in her music: she takes complex emotions and turns them into simple songs that anyone can listen to and love. In this case, she expertly captures the duality of infatuation — the thrill and the torment — and presents it in a way that is both personal and universally relatable.

Produced by Dan Nigro, who also co-wrote the track alongside Rodrigo and St. Vincent, the instrumentals blend elements of pop-rock and grunge, casting a haunting melody to perfectly compliment the lyrical content.

The day "obsessed" was released, Olivia also dropped the music video for it, much to the fans' delight. Directed by Mitch Ryan, the young singer finds herself in a hotel ballroom surrounded by competitive pageant queens, all of whom have dated the same guy she's in love with. The women's sashes bear inscriptions such as "Miss Thought She Was the One," "Miss Also Thought She Was the One," "Miss 2 Summers Ago," "Miss Mom's Favourite," and "Miss Still His 'Closest Friend'". Rodrigo dons a black dress in the clip, a stark contrast to the white gowns of the other women, visually indicating to viewers that she feels like an outsider in this emotional pageant.

GUTS SPILLED

After the 'drivers license' lore, of course many fans assumed the song was written about singer and actress Sabrina Carpenter, but there is more speculation that the song is about actress and model Madelyn Cline, who has been romantically linked to Olivia's ex Zack Bia.

Madelyn Cline

MADELYN CLINE

Madelyn Renee Cline (born December 21, 1997) is an American actress and model, best known for her roles as Sarah Cameron on the Netflix teen drama series Outer Banks (2020 – present) and as Whiskey in Rian Johnson's mystery film Glass Onion: A Knives Out Mystery (2022).

Following her split from her Outer Banks co-star Chase Stokes whom she dated from April 2020 to October 2021, the young star sparked romance rumours with Zack. Both Madelyn and Zack were photographed at the same October 2021 Lacoste fashion show in Paris and were seen grabbing lunch on multiple occasions.

The romance was short lived however, and as soon as the dating rumours died down between the pair, Zack Bia and Olivia Rodrigo were reported to have started things up again.

"girl i've always been"

This song is wildly different from not only the rest of the songs on *GUTS Spilled*, but also from any other song Olivia has ever released. "girl i've always been" explores the struggle between public persona and private self. Rodrigo's lyrics vividly capture the tension of trying to stay true to oneself while navigating the often-conflicting demands of the outside world. The lyrics suggest a confrontation between the singer and someone close to her, possibly a romantic partner, who accuses her of changing. Olivia refutes this by asserting that she remains the person she has always been, despite the accusations and the turbulence in her life.

The song almost has a folk-country vibe, with pop influences of course. Fans of her song "Can't Catch Me Now" from the Hunger Games: The Ballad of Songbirds and Snakes soundtrack would particularly enjoy "girl i've always been".

"scared of my guitar"

Olivia Rodrigo's "scared of my guitar" explores the emotional turmoil of being in a relationship devoid of genuine love and the fear of confronting one's true feelings. The guitar serves as a powerful metaphor for self-reflection and honesty. Rodrigo vividly describes feeling a 'pit' in her stomach, symbolizing the anxiety and unease brought on by her partner's presence. Despite trying to maintain a perfect image, she recognizes that something is fundamentally wrong, and this realization is overwhelming.

In the song, the guitar represents a tool for self-expression that she cannot deceive, unlike her partner. When she plays, she is forced to confront her true emotions, a daunting task she fears. The lyrics reveal her awareness of the disingenuous nature of her relationship, yet she continues to 'pretend that it's love' out of fear of the unknown and the possibility of not finding something better. The song poignantly captures the internal conflict between staying in a comfortable but flawed situation and taking the risk to pursue what is genuinely right.

This song is another perfect example of Olivia's knack for compelling storytelling.

Olivia Rodrigo ALL AMERICAN

"stranger"

Olivia Rodrigo's song "stranger" is a poignant reflection on personal growth and the process of moving on from a past relationship. Rodrigo's lyrics paint a vivid picture of waking up one day to a surprising realization: the overwhelming pain that once dominated her life has started to dissipate. This revelation is both startling and liberating, as it contradicts her earlier belief that the assurances of healing from others were just clichés.

The song delves into the transformation of the ex-lover from someone who was once an integral part of her life to a "stranger" she knows everything about. This shift in perspective highlights the distance she has put between her past self and her current state of completeness. The song acknowledges the complexity of letting go, expressing both gratitude for the shared experiences and a recognition of the necessity to move forward. Olivia's "stranger" touches on universal themes of love, loss, and self-discovery. The song resonates with anyone who has ever had to overcome the end of a significant relationship and found themselves stronger on the other side.

"so american"

It was only a matter of time before Olivia Rodrigo entered into her love song writing era. Her first two albums, *SOUR* and *GUTS*, featured a fair few heartbreak songs, but with the deluxe version of *GUTS*, Olivia is finally showing her fans her loved-up side.

Olivia Rodrigo's song "so american" vividly captures the intoxicating whirlwind of a new romance from the perspective of a young woman who is enamoured with her partner. The lyrics express a sense of youthful infatuation, where the protagonist is charmed by her lover's unique quirks and the way he makes her feel distinctly American. On the track, she repeats the word "lo-lo-lo-ve", suggesting a tentative admission of falling in love, and highlighting the excitement and uncertainty that often accompany the early stages of a relationship.

She mentions how her new flame drives on the right side of the road, leading listeners to believe that the guy in question is British. Ever since the release of the song, rumours have swirled surrounding the subject of the song, but the most popular and highly likely theory is that the song is about her new boyfriend Louis Partridge.

Louis Partridge

Louis Partridge is a 21-year-old British actor and model who has appeared in both Enola Holmes films alongside Millie Bobby Brown, and also played the notorious Sex Pistols bassist Sid Vicious in the FX series Pistol. Partridge was previously linked to actor Sydney Chandler, daughter of Friday Night Lights star Kyle Chandler, who had a small role in Don't Worry Darling.

Romance rumours between Olivia and Louis started swirling in late October 2023 when The Sun reported that Olivia travelled to London with her bestie, Conan Gray, to visit Louis and spend some time with him. An insider revealed that the pair allegedly met through mutual friends.

After a quiet month in November, Louis continued to fuel dating rumours when he showed up to support Olivia at iHeartRadio's Jingle Ball stop in New York at Madison Square Garden. He was spotted in the crowd with Rodrigo's best friends, Conan Gray and Madison Hu. Fans captured sweet moments on video like Partridge recording Rodrigo's

LOUIS PARTRIDGE

performance and singing along to "all-american b****." A day after the Jingle Ball, Louis was reportedly in the audience at Studio 8H to cheer Olivia on during her *Saturday Night Live* performance. They were also photographed at the show's after-party together and left in the same car.

But it wasn't until the 13th of December that fans finally got the proof they had long waited for. Pictures of Olivia and Louis sharing a passionate kiss in a gas station in New York took social media by storm, with many people praising the new couple for how cute they look.

Since their make out session, the young couple have been pictured going out on PDA-full dates. Louis continues to show his support for his girlfriend's music career, attending shows up and down the country.

On June 3rd, Louis Partridge posted a cute baby pic of himself dressed as a French man to celebrate his 21st birthday.

"One beer s'il vous plait 😎🎈,"

he captioned the post, while Olivia seemingly confirmed their relationship with a sweet comment, writing,

"welcome to the 21 club angel boy!!!! 🫶🫶🫶🫶".

GUTS SPILLED

Olivia dazzling at The O2, 2024

Olivia Rodrigo *ALL AMERICAN*

Olivia Rodrigo performs at the Wizink Center, Madrid, 2024

GUTS Tour

Olivia Rodrigo announced her highly anticipated *GUTS* World Tour on the 13th of September 2023. This extensive tour marks Olivia's first arena tour, following the success of her debut *SOUR* tour.

The shows kicked off on February 23rd, 2024, in Palm Springs, California, and will include 57 dates across North America and Europe, featuring stops in major cities such as Miami, Toronto, New York, London, Amsterdam, and Paris. It will conclude with back-to-back shows at the Kia Forum in Los Angeles on the 13th and 14th of August 2024.

The pop princess was hugely praised right from the get-go for her affordable ticket prices, ranging from $49.50 to $199.50, with various VIP packages available. Rodrigo has also introduced Silver Star Tickets, a special initiative offering cheaper $20 tickets to make her concerts even more accessible to fans, including those who may not have the financial means to afford higher-priced tickets. This democratizes the concert experience, promoting inclusivity and offering the chance for more people to see their favourite artist live. Additionally, demonstrating a commitment to affordability not only aligns with Olivia's values, but it also portrays her as an artist who genuinely cares about her fans' well-being.

Olivia's commitment to social causes doesn't just stop at cheaper ticket prices: she also announced that a portion of the proceeds from all ticket sales will go towards Olivia Rodrigo's Fund 4 Good.

Olivia Rodrigo ALL AMERICAN

GUTS Tour, Wizink Centre, Madrid 2024

Olivia Rodrigo ALL AMERICAN

GUTS TOUR

Opening night of the *GUTS* Tour, Palm Springs, California 2024

Fund 4 Good

In a video uploaded by her official TikTok fan, the 21-year-old singer explained to fans that she will be launching a brand-new initiative in support of reproductive rights, just as she was about to take the stage for the opening night of her GUTS World Tour.

"I'm so excited tonight it's the first night of the GUTS World Tour," she started the video. "Before I pop on stage, I wanted to come on here and tell you about something I'm really excited about, which is the Fund 4 Good, which is an initiative I'm launching as part of the GUTS World Tour." According to Rodrigo, the fund will support a myriad of programs that will work to protect the reproductive health freedom of women, girls, and people who menstruate. Some of the programs supported by the fund also reportedly tackle issues like girls' education and gender-based violence.

"A portion of all of the proceeds from the GUTS World Tour will go to the Fund 4 Good," Rodrigo continued to explain. "And for the North American leg of the GUTS World Tour, I'll be partnering with the National Network of Abortion Funds to help those impacted by health care barriers and getting the reproductive care they deserve."

The young popstar added that concertgoers will be able to learn more about the fund at the National Network of Abortion Funds tables set up at the GUTS tour stops throughout North America leg of her tour. "Thank you so much for supporting this cause that I care so deeply about," she concluded the video. "I can't wait to see you all on tour."

Hundreds of fans line up for the GUTS Tour Bus in New York's Meatpacking District

One of the standout elements of her performances is the emotional depth and authenticity she brings to the stage. For instance, during "pretty isn't pretty," Rodrigo's backup dancers use mirrors as props to highlight societal beauty standards, creating a powerful visual commentary on the pressures faced by young women. During her song "logical", a floating moon can be seen hovering over the performer, lending a magical feel to her concert.

Musically, Olivia's setlist balances her new material from the GUTS album with hits from her debut album SOUR. She also perfectly peppers her more upbeat songs throughout her show to keep her fans engaged and excited all along the night.

In addition to her compelling presence on stage, Olivia's shows also feature a diverse lineup of supporting acts for her fans to discover and love. One of them, in particular, gained a lot of popularity from collaborating with the young popstar and is on track to become the next big act in the music industry.

Olivia Rodrigo **ALL AMERICAN**

Kicking off the GUTS World Tour Palm Springs, California 2024

GUTS TOUR

Olivia Rodrigo ALL AMERICAN

Gwen Stefani and Olivia Rodrigo perform at Coachella 2024, Indio, California

GUTS TOUR

Olivia Rodrigo ALL AMERICAN

Olivia performing at the 3Arena, Dublin, 2024

Olivia Rodrigo ALL AMERICAN

Opening Act: Chappell Roan

Chappell Roan is an American singer-songwriter and innovative art-pop artist known for her emotive vocals and eclectic musical style. Born Kayleigh Rose Amstutz in Willard, Missouri, Roan began gaining attention with her distinctive blend of pop, indie, and electronic influences. Her music often explores themes of self-discovery, empowerment, and emotional vulnerability, marked by a theatrical and visually striking presentation, making her the perfect choice for Olivia Rodrigo's opening act on the *GUTS* Tour.

CHAPPELL ROAN

GUTS TOUR

Chappell Roan's career took a significant leap forward as she joined Olivia on the North American leg of the *GUTS* tour. As the opening act for 2023's most highly anticipated tour, Roan had the opportunity to perform her eclectic and emotionally charged music to packed arenas filled with Rodrigo's enthusiastic fans.

Since the start of the tour, Roan has seen a remarkable increase in her streaming numbers, with a 32% bump during the first weekend alone. This surge in interest is a testament to her captivating performances and the powerful connection she forges with new audiences. For fans of both artists, Roan's presence on the tour not only enhances the concert experience but also introduces a fresh, rising talent who is poised to make a lasting impact on the music scene.

Like many "overnight sensations," it took 26-year-old Chappell Roan years of hard work to reach her current success. Discovered a decade ago on YouTube by record executives, she moved from Missouri to Los Angeles with high hopes. However, her record deal eventually fell through, and by 2020, she found herself broke and back in her hometown, working as a barista at a drive-thru. Despite these setbacks, Roan never gave up on her music career. Her persistence paid off as ever since her contribution to the *GUTS* tour, the young singer seems destined to become the next big act in the music industry.

Olivia Rodrigo ALL AMERICAN

Olivia at The O2, 2024

Olivia Rodrigo performs 'Vampire' at the 66th Annual Grammy Awards, Los Angeles, 2024

GUTS TOUR

Style Icon

Olivia has quickly become one of the biggest names in music. At the same time, she has also made an impact in the style world with her Y2K-inspired looks, glamorous red-carpet outfits, and sustainable fashion.

Known for a blend of pop punk that transcends her music and drips into her wardrobe, Olivia is often seen sporting plaid, Dr. Martens, arm warmers and platform heels when performing. But it's her unique red carpet appearances that have cemented her as a genuine fashionista and tastemaker. Her looks are a testament to her evolving style, characterized by bold choices, elegant silhouettes, and a touch of youthful rebellion, whilst also seamlessly blending elements of current trends.

Here's a look at some of her most iconic fashion moments over the last few years:

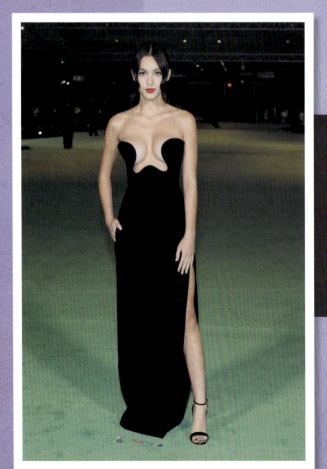

A chic black dress cut-out moment at The Academy Museum of Motion Pictures Opening Gala, Los Angeles, 2021

STYLE ICON

One of her standout moments was at the 2021 MTV Video Music Awards, where she wore a vintage-inspired Atelier Versace dress. The pink, corset-style gown featured a sweetheart neckline and intricate detailing, embodying old Hollywood glamour while maintaining a modern edge.

Olivia Rodrigo *ALL AMERICAN*

Another standout red carpet moment was at the 2021 BRIT Awards. Olivia wore a stunning neon-green Dior gown that turned heads and solidified her status as a fashion-forward artist. The daring colour choice and elegant silhouette demonstrated her ability to take risks while maintaining sophistication.

STYLE ICON

It's all feathers and lace whilst attending the 2021 Met Gala celebrating 'In America: A Lexicon of Fashion,' New York City, 2021

Her appearance at the 2022 Met Gala further showcased her fashion prowess. Rodrigo wore a shimmering purple (of course) Versace jumpsuit adorned with butterfly details, perfectly aligning with the gala's "In America: An Anthology of Fashion" theme. Her choice of outfit, complete with matching purple platform sandals, was both daring and glamorous and completely authentic to her and her brand

Olivia Rodrigo ALL AMERICAN

Olivia wearing a Vivienne Westwood gown to the Grammy Awards, 2022

STYLE ICON

At the Grammy Awards in 2022, Olivia opted for a sleek Vivienne Westwood gown in black with pink accents. The corseted bodice and elegant silhouette paid homage to classic fashion while maintaining a modern edge, and was in keeping with her pop-rock aesthetic.

Olivia's style influence extends beyond red carpets and music videos. Her everyday style, often shared on social media, has sparked numerous fashion trends among her fans. Pieces she wears frequently sell out, a testament to her impact on contemporary fashion. Items like her signature plaid skirts, oversized blazers, and vintage-inspired graphic tees have become staples in the wardrobes of many young fashion enthusiasts.

Rodrigo has a particular passion for thrifting, telling Vogue that she tries to "shop vintage, mostly" in addition to purchasing items on Depop or The RealReal. "I look for quality, and I like pieces that are kind of funky and weird," she told the publication. She uses her platform to advocate for sustainability and ethical fashion practices. By frequently opting for vintage and second-hand clothing, she encourages her followers to consider more sustainable options.

In 2021, Olivia partnered with the sustainable fashion brand Depop to create a curated collection of vintage pieces. This collaboration not only highlighted her commitment to sustainable fashion but also allowed fans to emulate her distinctive style.

Additionally, Olivia has been vocal about supporting designers from diverse backgrounds, using her influence to spotlight underrepresented voices in the fashion industry.

Olivia Rodrigo attends the Givenchy Womenswear Spring/Summer 2023 show during Paris Fashion Week, 2022.

Outro

In an industry where the trajectory from child star to pop sensation often follows a predictable path, Olivia Rodrigo stands out as a refreshing anomaly.

Her rise to fame, marked by authenticity, raw talent, and a distinct personal style, sets her apart from the typical Hollywood narrative. She continues to evolve as an artist and has a willingness to experiment with different musical styles, making her a refreshing and genuine presence in pop music. Olivia is also incredibly influential beyond her music: She uses her platform to advocate for issues she cares about, from mental health to social justice. Her openness about her own struggles with anxiety and self-doubt provides comfort and validation to many of her fans. Additionally, she has spoken out on various social and political issues, using her voice to raise awareness and inspire change. This commitment to advocacy sets her apart as a superstar who is not only talented but also deeply invested in making a positive impact.

Olivia's journey is a testament to the power of staying true to oneself and the impact of genuine artistry in a world often dominated by manufactured images. Every project she releases, and every collaboration she makes feels authentic and personal, and true to her values.

Olivia Rodrigo is not your typical superstar, as she constantly redefines what it means to be a modern-day icon.

The O2, 2024

OUTRO